NO SYMBOLS WHERE NONE INTENDED

A Catalogue of Books, Manuscripts,
and Other Material Relating to Samuel Beckett in the Collections
of the Humanities Research Center

Selected and Described by Carlton Lake

With the Assistance of Linda Eichhorn and Sally Leach

HUMANITIES RESEARCH CENTER • THE UNIVERSITY OF TEXAS AT AUSTIN

Title page: Illustration by Samuel Beckett from
his original manuscript of *Watt*. See entry no. 157.

Catalogue covers: from the original manuscript of *Watt*.

FOREWORD

"I don't find solitude agonizing, on the contrary. Holes in paper open and take me fathoms from anywhere." So wrote Samuel Beckett to Nancy Cunard on 26 January 1959. That land—"fathoms from anywhere"—only rarely and oneirically Ireland and not ever France, is like no other land in literature. It is consistent from work to work, as are the people who inhabit it. But within the homogeneity of background, of character, of theme, are subtle shadings of approach, of definition, of presentation that open up for the reader—or, in Beckett's plays, the viewer—vistas as varied as the range of human emotions. Hence the variety of responses to his work. For some, Beckett is one of the great comic writers of all time. For others, his is a tragic world, "bleak," "grim," even "unbearable." And for still others, he is a religious writer, his works a witness to the indomitable spirit of the Godhead-in-man.

It has done him no good to close one of his novels with the injunction "No symbols where none intended." The Beckett industry plows ahead and racks up, in the aggregate, more mileage per annum than that derived from the work of any other living writer—or from most of the dead. ("Dreadful, isn't it?" he says, shaking his head, with a wry smile.)

In doing honor to the man and the work, however one may define them, it would seem pointless to push claims, to struggle with rankings or to make sweeping historical assays. Most contemporary critics, here and abroad, would agree, however, that Samuel Beckett has given us, in English and in French, the most original work of our time. If, to many, that adds up to his being the greatest living writer, one of the greatest writers of this century, and one of the truly great writers of all time, well, so be it.

Exhibitions at the Humanities Research Center are drawn from HRC collections. That could be a limitation in some cases—if it were a question of Scott Fitzgerald, for example. But in the case of Samuel Beckett, we are fortunate indeed: we have more of the major manuscripts and correspondences than any other institution, and books *à gogo*.

What we have tried to do with these literary artifacts is not to make a year-by-year survey of Samuel Beckett's life or a definitive catalogue of his work; rather, to trace, as coherently as possible, the development, the progression—really, *le perpétuel devenir*—of this great and original work. We have let the books and manuscripts tell their own story, only sketching in background, where it seemed useful, in order to help them do so. In this respect, we have leaned heavily on the large groups of letters in our collections.

The result, we hope, will be to light up rather than to obscure the sources of the pleasure of reading, of hearing, of seeing Samuel Beckett.

CARLTON LAKE

See entry no. 338.

BEGINNINGS

Samuel Beckett was born on 13 April 1906 in Foxrock, near Dublin, into an upper-middle-class Protestant family. He took a degree in Modern Languages at Trinity College, Dublin, taught briefly in Belfast and then, under an exchange program between TCD and one of the more prestigious of the French *grandes écoles*, the Ecole Normale Supérieure, went to Paris as *lecteur d'anglais* for two years in the fall of 1928.

Jean Thomas, a colleague of Beckett's at "Normale Sup," remembered him as "tall, shy, reserved, with a clear, open gaze, bony, angular features, a tense and obstinate air, a stubborn brow, and a sense of restrained violence."

Beckett had plans to write a thesis on the poet Pierre-Jean Jouve, but soon after his arrival in Paris he gravitated, like other transplanted Irishmen before and since, toward the numinous figure of James Joyce. Introduced by Thomas MacGreevy, his predecessor in the Ecole Normale post, Beckett was soon accepted as one of the Joyce inner circle. Joyce's eyesight was failing and he called on Beckett to assist him in a variety of literary tasks. Joyce thought highly of Beckett and encouraged him to take part in the translation of the fragment of "Anna Livia Plurabelle"—a beautiful but difficult passage of "Work in Progress" (eventually to become *Finnegans Wake*)—which was published in *La Nouvelle Revue Française* for 1 May 1931.

During that period Adrienne Monnier and Sylvia Beach—whose book-shops, La Maison des Amis des Livres and Shakespeare and Company, faced each other across the lower end of the Rue de l'Odéon—saw a good deal of Beckett. They were struck, Adrienne once recalled, by his resemblance to the young Joyce as he appeared in certain photographs belonging to Sylvia, and they thought of him as a "new Stephen Dedalus." They found him "reticent," even "distant."

At the end of his two-year stint at the Ecole Normale Supérieure Beckett returned to Dublin, taught four terms at Trinity, then resigned, moving about a good deal in the process of finding his way as a writer. Early articles, poems, and stories of his were already beginning to appear in *Transition*, the avant-garde review edited by Eugene Jolas and sundry helpers, in Edward Titus's *This Quarter*, in Samuel Putnam's *The New Review*, in *The Dublin Magazine*, and elsewhere. He translated Rimbaud but nothing came of it. He worked at a novel, "Dream of Fair to Middling Women," which proved unpublishable. But just before his departure from Paris in 1930, he won a competition conducted by The Hours Press "for the best poem on Time" and the Press published his winning entry as a separate plaquette. The next year Chatto & Windus published his *Proust*. Three years later the same firm brought out a collection of his stories, *More Pricks Than Kicks*. By then, reviewing, translation assignments, literary journalism were incidental. He was the author of published books and, for the time being at least, had a buoyant confidence in his future as a writer.

OUR EXAGMINATION ROUND HIS FACTIFICATION FOR INCAMINATION OF WORK IN PROGRESS

BY

SAMUEL BECKETT, MARCEL BRION, FRANK BUDGEN,
STUART GILBERT, EUGENE JOLAS, VICTOR LLONA,
ROBERT MCALMON, THOMAS MCGREEVY,
ELLIOT PAUL, JOHN RODKER, ROBERT SAGE,
WILLIAM CARLOS WILLIAMS.

with

LETTERS OF PROTEST

BY

G. V. L. SLINGSBY AND VLADIMIR DIXON.

SHAKESPEARE AND COMPANY
SYLVIA BEACH
12, RUE DE L'ODÉON — PARIS
M CM XX IX

1

DEJEUNER "ULYSSE"

Jeudi 27 Juin 1929

PARIS — SOCIÉTÉ GÉNÉRALE
D'IMPRIMERIE ET D'ÉDITION
71, RUE DE RENNES - 1929

Hôtel Léopold
Les Vaux de Cernay

4

1. "Dante . . . Bruno . Vico . . Joyce." In *Our Exagmination Round His Factification for Incamination of Work in Progress* by Samuel Beckett, Marcel Brion, Frank Budgen, Stuart Gilbert, Eugene Jolas, Victor Llona, Robert McAlmon, Thomas MacGreevy, Elliot Paul, John Rodker, Robert Sage, William Carlos Williams, with Letters of Protest by G. V. L. Slingsby and Vladimir Dixon. Paris: Sylvia Beach, Shakespeare and Company, 1929. 8vo, original printed wrappers, uncut.

   96 large-paper copies were printed on *vergé d'Arches* (this copy unnumbered).
   Inscribed on the title page: "For Gabriel Zakin / very cordially his friend / Sylvia Beach / Paris 12.12.36."
   In the summer of 1928, Joyce and Sylvia Beach had begun to make plans for a volume of critical essays on Joyce's "Work in Progress." Joyce arranged to have articles written by his principal acolytes. Eleven of the twelve were thus legitimized. The article by William Carlos Williams was the only one that, unsolicited, came in over the transom. Joyce did, in fact, "stand behind those twelve Marshals more or less directing them what lines of research to follow . . ." as he wrote to Valery Larbaud on 30 July 1929. And so, to give the collection an air of impartiality, he and Sylvia Beach decided to add two "letters of protest." Vladimir Dixon, author of one of these, "A Litter to Mr. James Joyce" (it began, "Dear Mister Germ's Choice"), has been thought to be, in reality, Joyce himself. But a brief article by Thomas A. Goldwasser in the *James Joyce Quarterly* (Vol. XVI, No. 3, Spring 1979), identifies Dixon as a bona-fide writer, born in Russia of a Russian mother and an American father, and resident in Paris from 1923 until his death, in 1929. However, since all Dixon's other published work was written in Russian, the nagging question remains: Did Dixon actually write the pastiche or merely lend his name to it? Perhaps the truth lies somewhere in between. G. V. L. Slingsby, author of the other "protest," "Writes a Common Reader," was allegedly a woman journalist who frequented Shakespeare and Company, but was, in all likelihood, a *nom de plume* for Sylvia Beach.

2. _____. Another copy, also on large paper, with the signature of Frank Budgen, friend, biographer, and portraitist of James Joyce.

3. "Dante . . . Bruno . Vico . . Joyce." In *Transition: An International Quarterly for Creative Experiment*, No. 16–17 (June 1929). Paris: Principal Agency, Shakespeare and Co. Crown 8vo, original wrappers.

   Beckett's intention in establishing the idiosyncratic punctuation of the title of his article was to indicate the approximate time gap between the respective figures: 300 years from Dante to Bruno, 100 from Bruno to Vico, and 200 from Vico to Joyce. In the Table of Contents, *Transition's* proofreaders let him down, however, and inserted an additional century between Vico and Joyce.
   Jolas, an American of French and German extraction, fluent in the three languages, founded *Transition* as a vehicle for his "Revolution of the Word." Through Sylvia Beach he had met Joyce at the end of 1926. When he heard Joyce read the early portion of his "Work in Progress"

and, soon after, read more of it himself from a typescript Joyce asked Sylvia Beach to lend him, his mission became apparent: he would publish the work serially as the focus of his revolution. The first issue appeared in April 1927. His coeditor was Elliot Paul, an American novelist and music critic. As time went on, Jolas's editorial voice became the dominant one: the masthead of this issue lists Jolas as Editor, followed by a quintet of "Advisory Editors": Harry Crosby, Stuart Gilbert, Matthew Josephson, Elliot Paul, and Robert Sage.

The issue contains, also, Beckett's short story "Assumption."

4. Menu of the luncheon—the *Déjeuner "Ulysse"*—given by Adrienne Monnier on Thursday, 27 June 1929 at the Hôtel Léopold in Les Vaux de Cernay, not far from Versailles, to mark, somewhat tardily, the publication of the French translation of *Ulysses* nearly five months earlier, as well as the silver anniversary of Bloomsday (June 16).

Among the invited guests—in addition to Joyce and Nora—were Paul Valéry, Edouard Dujardin, Jules Romains, and their respective consorts; Philippe Soupault, Léon-Paul Fargue, Sylvia Beach, Paul-Emile Bécat and his wife, Marie (Adrienne Monnier's sister); Giorgio Joyce and his fiancée Helen Fleischman; Pierre de Lanux, once secretary to André Gide; Ludmila Savitzky, translator of *Portrait of the Artist*; André Chamson, Marie Scheikévitch, who had been one of Proust's most intimate women friends; Thomas MacGreevy, and Samuel Beckett.

In a long letter to Valery Larbaud written from the Imperial Hotel at Torquay at the end of July, Joyce gave some of the highlights of the luncheon. After scolding Larbaud, lightly and by indirection, for his absence—he, the Abbé Morel, Stuart Gilbert, Edmond Jaloux, and Gide were the conspicuous absentees in Joyce's recital—Joyce told him about "two riotous young Irishmen . . . one of [whom] fell deeply under the influence of beer, wine spirits, liqueurs, fresh air, movement and feminine society and was ingloriously abandoned by the Wagonette in one of those temporary palaces which are inseparably associated with the memory of the Emperor Vespasian." No Irish names were mentioned.

The menu bears the autograph signatures of Joyce and a number of the other guests. It is the copy given to Madame Marie Scheikévitch.

5. "Delta" by Eugenio Montale, "Landscape" by Raffaello Franchi, and "The Home-Coming" by Giovanni Comisso. Translated from the Italian by Samuel Beckett. In *This Quarter*, Vol. II, No. 4 (April-May-June 1930). Paris: Edward W. Titus. Crown 8vo, wrappers, uncut.

"The present issue is, in large part, devoted to translations from contemporary Italian literature . . . in each instance the work of experts chosen with scrupulous care." Three of the translations, as listed above, are credited to "S. B. Beckett."

In an editorial foreword titled "Transit Transition," Edward Titus took note of the rumored impending demise of *Transition*. "Its courage was always admirable, if at times misdirected. Its chief merit, to our mind, lay in the opportunities it afforded, liberally and sincerely, to young writers, often utterly indisciplined, anarchic, and ill-disposed to all that appertains to legitimately publishable literary expression, to give vent in print to their supposedly artistic troubles and aspirations."

6. "For Future Reference" [poem]. In *Transition*, No. 19-20 (June 1930). Paris: Principal Agency, Shakespeare and Co. Crown 8vo, original wrappers, uncut.

In this issue, with Harry Crosby dead and Matthew Josephson and Elliot Paul otherwise occupied, only two Advisory Editors remain: the faithful Stuart Gilbert and Robert Sage. Over Sage's signature this number carried a "Farewell to *Transition*: A Letter to Eugene Jolas from Robert Sage." Despite Sage's premature burst of nostalgia, the magazine managed to survive for another seven issues.

7. "Whoroscope." Autograph manuscript [1930], 6 pp., folio, written in ink on stationery from the Hotel Bristol at Carcassonne.

With an autograph note in Beckett's hand: "This is the original MS. of my first published poem. Samuel Beckett." Page 6 contains the autograph manuscript of the sonnet "At last I find in my confused soul," published in a variant form in "Sedendo et Quiescendo" (see No. 22).

At the suggestion of his friend Thomas MacGreevy, Beckett, then twenty-four years old, wrote "Whoroscope" in a matter of hours, as a last-minute entry in the contest sponsored by Nancy Cunard and Richard Aldington for a poem of not more than 100 lines on the subject of Time. The prize was £10 and publication by Cunard's Hours Press. Descartes had been much on Beckett's mind, and from notes on his readings he drew the makings of this witty, arcane poem of 98 lines which both mystified and delighted the sponsors. At their suggestion Beckett added two pages of explanatory notes.

7, 7a

11

7a. "Whoroscope." Typed manuscript [1930], 3 pp., folio.

In green wrappers, cover marked in red crayon in Nancy Cunard's hand, "Typescript of 'Whoroscope' by Samuel Beckett. The Hours Press edition was set from this in the summer of 1930 in Paris."

Autograph note, in the same hand, on page 1: "Typescript from which the HOURS PRESS set this poem of Samuel Beckett in Paris, Summer of 1930."

8. *Whoroscope.* Paris: The Hours Press, 1930. 8vo, original printed wrappers, uncut.

With the original white wrap-around slip stating: "This Poem was awarded the £10 prize for the best poem on Time in the competition judged by Richard Aldington and Nancy Cunard at The Hours Press, and is published in an edition of 100 signed copies at 5 s. and 200 unsigned at 1 s. This is also Mr. Samuel Beckett's first separately published work."

This is Beckett's presentation copy to Nancy Cunard, inscribed on the limitation page: "With tante belle / cose for Nancy – / Samuel" and beneath this, in Cunard's hand, "Hours Press / Own Set."

A tipped-in letter to "Bien Chère Nancy" dated 26.1.59 gives Beckett's recollections of entering "Whoroscope" in the competition: "Whoroscope was indeed entered for your competition and the prize of I think 1000 francs. I knew nothing about it till afternoon of last day of entry, wrote first half before dinner, had a guzzle of salad and Chambertin at the Cochon de Lait, went back to the Ecole and finished it about three in the morning. Then walked down to the Rue Guénégaud and put it in your box. That's how it was and them were the days."

9. _____. Copy No. 84, inscribed on the limitation page: "Samuel Beckett sent the typescript / of this poem to me in the summer of / 1930. Of the 100 or so poems sent in for / the 'Best poem on Time,' it was by far the / best—unique indeed! And so I rejoice / in being the first to have published anything / of his. Dear Mr. Schwartz you have / my best thoughts! / Nancy Cunard / London. Jan. 19, 1956."

10. _____. Another copy, signed by Samuel Beckett, and inscribed in Nancy Cunard's hand "for / Lytton Strachey."

11. _____. Another copy, inscribed: "for / M. J. McManus / from / Sam Beckett / 30.11.36," with a correction by Beckett of the typographical error on page 2.

11a. Photograph of Nancy Cunard by Cecil Beaton, inscribed in ink, lower right, by Beaton. At lower left, in Nancy Cunard's hand, the phrase "A quoi?," a reference to Alfred de Musset's *A quoi rêvent les jeunes filles?* On the back Cunard has written a dithyrambic answer to her own question, centering around the figure of her current lover, the left-wing writer [André] Thirion.

a chère Nancy

Thanks for your letter and the nice things you say about
t jolly evening in Sloane Square.

horoscope was indeed entered for your competition and
 prize of I think 1000 francs. I knew nothing about it
 afternoon of last day of entry, wrote first half before
er, had a guzzle of salad and Chambertin at the Cochon
ait, went back to the Ecole and finished it about three
the morning. Then walked down to the Rue Guénégaud and put
n your box. That's how it was and them were the days.

 was very disappointed we did not meet in London. I had
ief and exhausting time there trying to get things the
 I wanted, right or wrong. I was very pleased with Krapp,
 not with Endgame, which needed another week's rehearsal.

You wouldn't know where to live these days, or why. Here
 the best I have, not a sound and the Ile de France bowing
lf out. I don't find solitude agonizing, on the contrary.
es in paper open and take me fathoms from anywhere.

Much love and vivement les retrouvailles.

300 *copies of this Poem
have been printed, of
which* 100 *copies are
signed by the author.*

This is N̲i̲t̲h̲ *rank with*
con for Nancy —
Samuel

HOURS PRESS
OWN SET

8

This Poem was awarded the £ 10 *prize for the
best poem on* TIME *in the competition judged by
Richard Aldington and Nancy Cunard at*
THE HOURS PRESS, *and is published in an
edition of* 100 *signed copies at* 5 *s.
and* 200 *unsigned at* 1 *s.*

This is also Mr. Samuel Beckett's first separately published work.

11a

12

14

12. "From the Only Poet to a Shining Whore: For Henry Crowder to Sing." In *Henry-Music* by Henry Crowder. Paris: Hours Press, 1930. Folio, original pictorial boards from a montage of photographs by Man Ray in which Nancy Cunard's ivory bracelets figure prominently.

> One of 100 numbered copies, signed by Henry Crowder.
> In addition to Beckett's poem, Henry Crowder set to music poems by Nancy Cunard, Richard Aldington, Walter Lowenfels, and Harold Acton.
> Crowder played piano with an American jazz band, Eddie Smith and his Alabamians, on tour in Europe. He met Nancy Cunard in Venice in 1928, became her lover, and probably did more than anyone else to change the focus of her life.
> From the library of Nancy Cunard.

13. *Proust.* London: Chatto & Windus, 1931. 12mo, original pictorial boards.

> First edition.
> Inscribed on the second flyleaf: "for my friend / Ernie O'Malley / Dublin June 1946 / Sam Beckett."
> In this study Beckett eschews all reference "to the legendary life and death of Marcel Proust . . . to the garrulous old dowager of the Letters . . . to the poet . . . to the author of the Essays." His intention: "to examine in the first place that double-headed monster of damnation and salvation—Time."

14. _____. Another copy, inscribed on the verso of the half-title: "for / Jake Schwartz / Sam Beckett / This essay was / commissioned by / Chatto & Windus when / I was at the / Ecole Normale Supérieure – / Paris, 1929."

15. James Joyce. "Anna Livie Plurabelle." Translated by Samuel Beckett, Alfred Perron [*sic*], Ivan Goll, Eugene Jolas, Paul L. Léon, Adrienne Monnier, and Philippe Soupault, in collaboration with the author. In *La Nouvelle Revue Française,* (1 May 1931). 8vo, original printed wrappers, uncut.

> Large-paper copy.
> In his preface to these excerpts from the translation (the first third of *Anna Livia* plus the last two pages), Philippe Soupault writes that a first draft had been prepared by Samuel Beckett, assisted by Alfred Péron, and that a revision of that version was done, under Joyce's supervision, by Paul Léon, Eugene Jolas, and Ivan Goll. Then Joyce, Léon, and Soupault, over a period of fifteen weekly sessions lasting three hours each, revised the revision. That version was submitted to Jolas and Adrienne Monnier. Jolas sent his comments from Austria, Adrienne Monnier gave hers in person, and the team incorporated their changes—along with others made in the meantime by Joyce and Soupault—into the final version.

16. Invitation from Adrienne Monnier to "Monsieur [George] Reavey" to attend the Joyce evening at her bookshop, La Maison des Amis des Livres, Thursday, 26 March 1931, at nine o'clock.

The program included a recording of Joyce reading a fragment of "Anna Livia Plurabelle" and a reading by Adrienne Monnier of the French translation prepared by Beckett and others.

17. "Hell Crane to Starling," "Casket of Pralinen for a Daughter of a Dissipated Mandarin," "Text," and "Yoke of Liberty." In *The European Caravan: An Anthology of the New Spirit in European Literature.* Compiled and edited by Samuel Putnam, Maida Castelhun Darnton, George Reavey, and J. Bronowski. With special introductions by André Berge, Massimo Bontempelli, Jean Cassou, and E. Giménez Cabellero. Part I. France, Spain, England and Ireland. New York: Brewer, Warren & Putnam, 1931. 8vo, original cloth.

The introductory notice to these four poems states that "S. B. Beckett is the most interesting of the younger Irish writers. . . . He has a great knowledge of Romance literature, is a friend of Rudmose-Brown and of Joyce, and has adapted the Joyce method to his poetry with original results. His impulse is lyric, but has been deepened through this influence and the influence of Proust and of the historic method."

In a 1932 letter to George Reavey, Beckett's (and Reavey's) friend Thomas MacGreevy wrote: "You should tell Bronowski [editor of the "England and Ireland" section of *The European Caravan*] that it was a dirty trick on Beckett to say he was a friend of Rudmose-Brown. (But not from me)."

The point of MacGreevy's remark is clouded by the fact that [Thomas] Rudmose-Brown was the professor at Trinity under whom Beckett took first-class honors in French and Italian and who encouraged him to make his first trips to France, helped him in the matter of his appointment to the Ecole Normale Supérieure, made him his principal assistant after his return from his Paris post, and continued to encourage him, even after Beckett had left Trinity, with half of his teaching appointment uncompleted.

18. "Return to the Vestry" [poem]. In *The New Review: An International Notebook for the Arts Published from Paris.* Edited by Samuel Putnam. Vol. I, No. 3 (August-September-October 1931). Folio, original printed wrappers, uncut.

19. "Text." In *The New Review.* Edited by Samuel Putnam and Peter Neagoe. Vol. I, No. 4 (Winter 1931–32). Folio, original printed wrappers, uncut.

Beckett's poem was printed by "Courtesy of *The European Caravan*," with one typographical error introduced by courtesy of *The New Review*.

This issue carried also a poem by Beckett's friend George Reavey—"Faust, Fauna, and Spring." In an undated letter to Reavey, Thomas MacGreevy wrote, "I've just read the F. F. & Spring section in the N[ew] R[eview]. It is powerful, lofty and has many beautiful images. Against it, (and not against it, because I think I understand it) I would only say that I think the tendency of the day is towards a clear indication of one's meaning. I shouldn't I mean merely think I understand. I should be quite certain—assuming that I am a tolerably intelligent reader. This doesn't really worry me for you and Beckett. It does worry me a bit for Joyce and the fate of *Work in Progress* when it does finally appear. For Joyce is not young and you and Beckett are and will evolve towards clear statement."

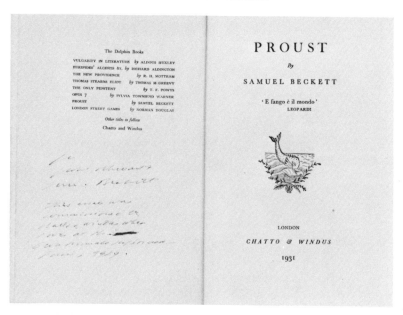

14

19ᵉ ANNÉE Nº 212   1ᵉʳ MAI 1931

LA NOUVELLE
REVUE FRANÇAISE

nrf

LA MAISON DES AMIS DES LIVRES
7, Rue de l'Odéon – PARIS-VIᵉ
Tél. : Littré 25-05

JEUDI 26 MARS 1931
à 9 heures précises du soir

SÉANCE CONSACRÉE A JAMES JOYCE

JOYCE ET LE PUBLIC FRANÇAIS
Causerie par ADRIENNE MONNIER

FRAGMENT
DE " ANNA LIVIA PLURABELLE "
lu en anglais par JAMES JOYCE
(Lecture enregistrée)

PRÉSENTATION
PAR PHILIPPE SOUPAULT
de la traduction française inédite d'un fragment
de " ANNA LIVIE PLURABELLE "

Lecture par ADRIENNE MONNIER de ce fragment
traduit par : SAMUEL BECKETT, ALFRED
PERRON, PAUL L. LÉON, IVAN GOLL, EUGÈNE
JOLAS, A. MONNIER et PHILIPPE SOUPAULT

15 16

20. "Alba." In *The Dublin Magazine: A Quarterly Review of Literature, Science and Art.* Vol. VI, No. 4, New Series (October-December 1931). [New York, 1967].

An early version of the poem collected in 1935, with variants, in *Echo's Bones and Other Precipitates.*

21. "Alba." Translated from the English by A. R. Peron [*sic*]. In *Soutes: Revue de Culture Révolutionnaire Internationale,* No. 9 (1938). 12mo, original wrappers, uncut.

This translation by Beckett's friend Alfred Péron follows very closely Beckett's text. The story had been written at Trinity during the period when Beckett first knew Péron, who had come there as French lecturer under the same exchange agreement with the Ecole Normale Supérieure that, two years later, took Beckett to Paris.

Beckett has signed his name under the printed signature at the end of his poem.

22. "Sedendo et Quiesciendo" [*sic*]. In *Transition,* No. 21 (March 1932). The Hague: Servire Press. Crown 8vo, original pictorial wrappers, from a design by Hans Arp.

"Sedendo et Quiescendo" is an early form of a passage from Beckett's unpublished novel "Dream of Fair to Middling Women," parts of which emerged later in his collection of short stories, *More Pricks Than Kicks.*

This issue contains, also, one of *Transition*'s most eloquent and characteristic pronouncements, "Poetry is Vertical," a manifesto signed by Hans Arp, Samuel Beckett, Carl Einstein, Eugene Jolas, Thomas MacGreevy, Georges Pelorson, Theo Rutra [Eugene Jolas], James J. Sweeney, and Ronald Symond. From the casual opening note of Léon-Paul Fargue's lines:

> On a été trop horizontal, j'ai
> envie d'être vertical

to the clarion call of the climax:

> the synthesis of a true collectivism is made possible by a community of spirits who aim at the construction of a new mythological reality

it is a heady journey through "telluric depths upward toward the illumination of a collective reality and a totalistic universe," a journey which could only have been conducted—orchestrated?—by Eugene Jolas.

■■■■ POETRY IS VERTICAL ■■■■

On a été trop horizontal, j'ai
envie d'être vertical. — Léon Paul Fargue.

In a world ruled by the hypnosis of positivism, we proclaim the autonomy of the poetic vision, the hegemony of the inner life over the outer life.

We reject the postulate that the creative personality is a mere factor in the pragmatic conception of progress, and that its function is the delineation of a vitalistic world.

We are against the renewal of the classical ideal, because it inevitably leads to a decorative reactionary conformity, to a factitious sense of harmony, to the sterilisation of the living imagination.

We believe that the orphic forces should be guarded from deterioration, no matter what social system ultimately is triumphant.

Esthetic will is not the first law. It is in the immediacy of the ecstatic revelation, in the a-logical movement of the psyche, in the organic rhythm of the vision that the creative act occurs.

The reality of depth can be conquered by a voluntary mediumistic conjuration, by a stupor which proceeds from the irrational to a world beyond a world.

The transcendental 'I' with its multiple stratifications reaching back millions of years is related to the entire history of mankind, past and present, and is brought to the surface with the hallucinatory irruption of images in the dream, the daydream, the mystic-gnostic trance, and even the psychiatric condition.

The final disintegration of the 'I' in the creative act is made possible by the use of a language which is a mantic instrument, and which does not hesitate to adopt a revolutionary attitude toward word and syntax, going even so far as to invent a hermetic language, if necessary.

Poetry builds a nexus between the 'I' and the 'you' by

leading the emotions of the sunken, telluric depths upward toward the illumination of a collective reality and a totalistic universe.

The synthesis of a true collectivism is made possible by a community of spirits who aim at the construction of a new mythological reality.

Hans Arp, Samuel Beckett,
Carl Einstein, Eugene Jolas,
Thomas McGreevy, Georges
Pelorson, Theo Rutra, James
J. Sweeney, Ronald Symond

22

23. [Translations by Beckett]. In *This Quarter*, Vol. V, No. 1 (September 1932). Crown 8vo, original printed wrappers, uncut.

Surrealist Number, with the signature of the poet and psychotherapist Carl Rakosi on the front cover.

The works translated by Beckett comprise "The Free Union," "Lethal Relief," and "Factory" (from *Soluble Fish* by André Breton); "Lady Love," "Out of Sight in the Direction of My Body," "Scarcely Disfigured," "The Invention," "Definition," "A Life Uncovered or The Human Pyramid," "The Queen of Diamonds," "Do Thou Sleep," "Second Nature," "Scene," "All-Proof: Universe Solitude," and "Confections" by Paul Eluard; "The Possessions," "Simulation of Mental Debility Essayed," "Simulation of General Paralysis Essayed," and "Simulation of the Delirium of Interpretation Essayed" by André Breton and Paul Eluard; "Everyone Thinks Himself Phoenix . . ." by René Crevel.

The ever-modest Edward Titus, whose succulent prose style establishes him as the ranking euphuist among Paris expatriates of the period, published this special surrealist number "for fear of growing *blasé* with encomiums on the quality of the material *This Quarter* has printed consistently during the three years of the present Editor's incumbency. . . . Possessing ourselves not a germ of surrealist proclivities, we may, however, say this, that if, by the evocation of the unconscious or subliminal self, poems are produced such as some of those printed in this issue, the day may come when the need of re-examination of every known definition of art—certainly of the art of poetry at least—will force itself upon us.

"We shall not speak of the difficulties experienced in putting the material placed at our disposal into English, but we cannot refrain from singling out Mr. Samuel Beckett's work for special acknowledgement. His rendering of the Eluard and Breton poems in particular is characterizable only in superlatives."

André Breton, founder and leader of the surrealist movement, had been retained as Guest Editor. Titus gave him *carte blanche* but then edited his texts of "such . . . topics as might not be in honeyed accord with Anglo-American censorship usages." Breton's happiness, he said, was "not complete."

23a. Group photograph, by Man Ray, of many of the principal members of the surrealist movement. Lower row: Tristan Tzara, Salvador Dali, Paul Eluard, Max Ernst, René Crevel. Upper row: Man Ray, Jean Arp, Yves Tanguy, André Breton. On the back Man Ray has identified, in pencil, the cast of characters.

24. "Dante and the Lobster." In *This Quarter*, Vol. V, No. 2 (December 1932). 8vo, original printed wrappers, uncut.

Beckett had submitted "Dante and the Lobster" for a short-story competition—the Heinemann 50 Guinea Award—advertised on the cover of the four previous issues of *This Quarter*. The story was accepted for publication, but the judges—Titus, Somerset Maugham, and a representative of the Heinemann firm—awarded the prize to a "Mr. Leslie Reid" for his story "Across the Heath."

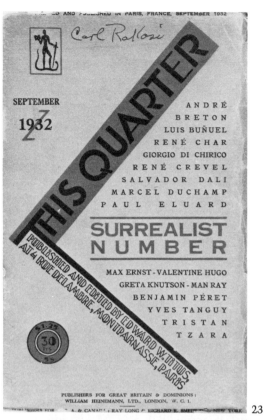

Carl Rakosi

PRINTED AND PUBLISHED IN PARIS, FRANCE, SEPTEMBER 1932

SEPTEMBER
1932

THIS QUARTER

ANDRÉ
BRETON
LUIS BUÑUEL
RENÉ CHAR
GIORGIO DI CHIRICO
RENÉ CREVEL
SALVADOR DALI
MARCEL DUCHAMP
PAUL ELUARD

**SURREALIST
NUMBER**

MAX ERNST - VALENTINE HUGO
GRETA KNUTSON - MAN RAY
BENJAMIN PÉRET
YVES TANGUY
TRISTAN
TZARA

PUBLISHED AND EDITED BY EDWARD W. TITUS
AU 4 RUE DELAMBRE, MONTPARNASSE, PARIS

$1.25
30 FRS
5/-

PUBLISHERS FOR GREAT BRITAIN & DOMINIONS :
WILLIAM HEINEMANN, LTD., LONDON, W. C. 1.

PUBLISHERS FOR U. S. A. & CANADA : RAY LONG & RICHARD R. SMITH, INC., NEW YORK

23

23a

21

25. "Home Olga." In *Contempo*, Vol. III, No. 13 (15 February 1934). Folio, unbound sheets, uncut.

Contempo's Joyce issue, edited by Stuart Gilbert, included this celebratory acrostic poem built on the ten letters of James Joyce's name. Other Joycean celebrants, in addition to Beckett and Stuart Gilbert, included Jolas, Padraic Colum, William van Wyck, Richard Thoma, and Bennett Cerf.

Contempo was edited at Chapel Hill principally by Milton Abernethy and (in the beginning) Anthony Buttitta. The first number was dated May 1931, and the magazine was scheduled to come out biweekly—subscription price one dollar a year. Much of its material— most of it from name authors—was free. Among its contributors and contributing editors were Ezra Pound, William Faulkner, James Joyce, Wallace Stevens, Nathanael West, William Carlos Williams, D. H. Lawrence, Hart Crane, E. E. Cummings, Erskine Caldwell, James T. Farrell, Louis Zukofsky, Boris Pasternak, John Dos Passos, Louis Aragon, and scores of others—"every writer of note," according to Buttitta, "but Hemingway, Wolfe, and Fitzgerald."

26. René Crevel. "La Négresse des Bordels." Typed manuscript, 8 pp., folio.

With autograph corrections in Crevel's hand.

Beckett translated this article for Nancy Cunard's 1934 anthology, *Negro*, as "The Negress in the Brothel" (pp. 581–583).

Later in 1934 Crevel abandoned the surrealist movement in favor of the French Communist Party and the following year committed suicide in the fashion he had envisaged in his novel *Détours*.

27. Henri Lavachery. "Essay on Styles in the Statuary of the Congo." Typed manuscript [1932], 14 pp., 4to.

With autograph corrections and additions in Nancy Cunard's hand. Together with a carbon copy of the French original, with some emendations.

An autograph note, in Nancy Cunard's hand, reads "(translated from the French [for *Negro*] by Samuel Beckett)."

28. Benjamin Péret. "Noirs sur blancs. Introduction. Fragment." Typed manuscript, signed, 10 pp., folio.

With autograph corrections and additions throughout in Péret's hand.

This text by one of the leading surrealist poets was translated by Beckett for *Negro* as "Black and White in Brazil" (pp. 510–514).

29. Charles Ratton. "The Ancient Bronzes of Black Africa." Typed manuscript [1932], 8 pp., 4to.

With an autograph note in Nancy Cunard's hand: "translated from the French [for *Negro*] by Samuel Beckett."

30. *Negro. Anthology Made by Nancy Cunard 1931–1933.* London: Nancy Cunard at Wishart & Co., 1934. Folio, original black cloth lettered in red.

Edition limited to 1,000 copies, but 150 extra copies were printed and distributed as gifts to the 150 collaborators, one of whom was Samuel Beckett, who translated nineteen of the articles into English.

This is Nancy Cunard's copy, with an autograph note in her hand, giving the publication date as 15 February, and adding: "My own copy. Nancy Cunard. Oct 1941. London. What remained of the whole edition has been destroyed by bombs and fire last year (Sept.), save 10 copies, saved by E. E. Wishart, as if in prevision." The book was "Dedicated to / Henry Crowder / my first Negro friend."

31. *More Pricks Than Kicks.* London: Chatto and Windus, 1934. 12mo, original cloth.

First edition, of which 1,500 copies were printed.

Inscribed by Beckett on the title page: "for John & Evelyn [Kobler] / Affectionately / from Sam / Paris April 1966."

The stories that make up this work, strongly autobiographical, first appeared two years earlier in the guise of a novel, "Dream of Fair to Middling Women," which is still unpublished.

Chatto and Windus printed 1,500 copies of *More Pricks*, but managed to sell only 500, thereby losing all interest in further publishing projects involving Beckett.

32. *More Pricks Than Kicks.* London: Calder & Boyars, 1966. 4to, original printed covers, stapled.

"Special edition Hors Commerce for Scholars."

Inscribed on the title page: "With love from Sam / for John and Evelyn [Kobler] / Paris May 67."

For years Beckett resisted publishers' requests that *More Pricks* be brought back into print. Finally he allowed John Calder to bring out a mimeographed edition for the use of the growing army of Beckett scholars.

33. *More Pricks Than Kicks.* London: Calder & Boyars (1970). 12mo, loose in sheets, uncut.

Author's proofs of the third edition with corrections in ink in Beckett's hand.

Inscribed on the half-title: "for John [Kobler] with / love from Sam / Paris June / 1970."

Four years after the "Special Hors-Commerce Edition," Calder & Boyars brought out this edition in their usual manner—one issue at a nominal price and one limited and signed.

34. *More Pricks Than Kicks.* London: Calder & Boyars (1970). 12mo, original leather-backed cloth boards, all edges gilt, in cloth slipcase. One of "a specially bound and limited edition of 100 copies . . . numbered, signed by the author."

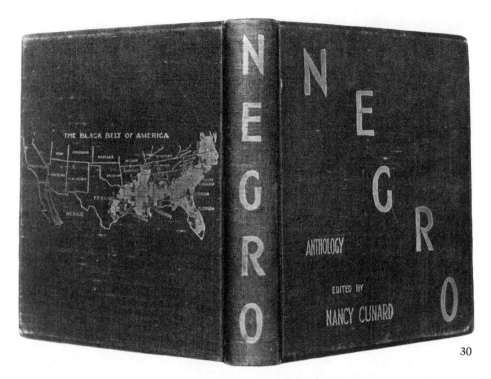

30

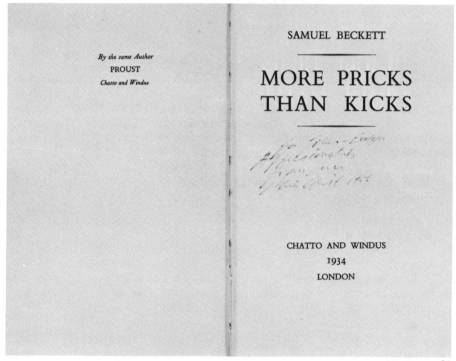

31

34a. "Jem Higgins' Love-Letter to the Alba." In *New Durham* (June 1965). 4to, full cloth, original decorative wrappers bound in.

A fragment from Beckett's unpublished novel "Dream of Fair to Middling Women" (ca. 1932). It is preceded by a critical essay on Beckett's work, entitled "Samuel Beckett; or, the Morbid Dread of Sphinxes," by John Fletcher.

35. [Untitled review of Rainer Maria Rilke's *Poems*.] Translated by J. B. Lishmann [*sic*]. In *The Criterion: A Quarterly Review Edited by T. S. Eliot*, Vol. XIII, No. 53 (July 1934). 8vo, original printed wrappers, uncut.

This was the only article Beckett published in Eliot's magazine. Their mutual friend Thomas MacGreevy, who had published a book on Eliot in 1931, may have been responsible for the assignment. If so, his influence did not endure.
Beckett characterizes Rilke's verse as "breathless petulance," an "overstatement of the solitude which [Rilke] cannot make his element." In his view, Rilke sees himself as interchangeable with God, a stance Beckett terms a "turmoil of self-deception . . . a childishness to which German writers seem specially prone": sentiments and phrasing hardly designed to endear him to Mr. Eliot.

36. "Gnome." In *The Dublin Magazine*, Vol. IX, No. 3, New Series (July–September 1934). Small 4to, original printed wrappers, uncut and unopened.

A poem of four lines, signed "Sam Beckett."
This issue of *The Dublin Magazine* contains also Beckett's review of Thomas MacGreevy's *Poems*, under the title "Humanistic Quietism." For Beckett, MacGreevy's work evolves from a "nucleus of endopsychic clarity, uttering itself in the prayer that is a spasm of awareness. . . ."
"To the mind that has raised itself to the grace of humility," Beckett writes, "prayer is no more (no less) than an act of recognition. A nod, even a wink. The flag dipped in Ave, not hauled down in Miserere. This is the adult mode of prayer syntonic to Mr. MacGreevy, the unfailing salute to *his* significant from which the fire is struck and the poem kindled, and kindled to a radiance without counterpart in the work of contemporary poets writing in English, who tend to eschew as understatement anything and everything between brilliance and murk."
When Beckett reached the Ecole Normale Supérieure in Paris in 1928 on the exchange fellowship that had been awarded him, he found MacGreevy—the previous recipient—still there. They became close friends and the letters Beckett addressed to MacGreevy for the rest of his life (MacGreevy died in 1967) are the richest source we have of information about Beckett's activities, his aspirations and disappointments, during those four decades.

VOLUME XIII NUMBER LIII

THE CRITERION

A QUARTERLY REVIEW
EDITED BY T. S. ELIOT

July 1934

CONTENTS

INITIATION ON A MOUNTAIN	WILLIAM BUTLER YEATS
THE FRIGATE PELICAN	MARIANNE MOORE
MODERN PROSE STYLE	BONAMY DOBREE
BANDITTI	HUGH SYKES DAVIES
JOHN MARSTON	THEODORE SPENCER
FOUR POEMS	CHARLES MADGE
JAPANESE PRIMITIVE	W. W. WINKWORTH
THE VOYAGE	FREDERIC PROKOSCH

A COMMENTARY
BY THE EDITOR

ART CHRONICLE	ROGER HINKS
MUSIC CHRONICLE	PHILIP F. RADCLIFFE
FRENCH CHRONICLE	MONTGOMERY BELGION

CORRESPONDENCE: from the ENGLISH ASSOCIATION.

BOOKS OF THE QUARTER: CAN WE LIMIT WAR?: (page 657) reviewed by MAJOR GEN. SIR E. D. SWINTON. THE LETTERS OF STEPHEN GARDINER: (page 659) reviewed by THE REV. CHARLES SMYTH. THE ORIGINS OF MODERN SPAIN: (page 662) reviewed by ORLO WILLIAMS. THE WORKER'S POINT OF VIEW: (page 665) reviewed by STEPHEN SPENDER. RELIGIONS AND COSMIC BELIEFS OF CENTRAL POLYNESIA: (page 668) reviewed by K. DE B. CODRINGTON. WINTER IN MOSCOW: (page 670) reviewed by JOHN COURNOS. BOOKS ABOUT POETRY: (page 673) a review by T. C. WILSON. FIRST RUSSIA THEN TIBET: (page 675) reviewed by ADRIAN STOKES. WAYS AND CROSSWAYS: (page 678) reviewed by ASHLEY SAMPSON. LA PHILOSOPHIE DE NEWMAN: (page 680) reviewed by ALGAR THOROLD. JOYCE AND THE MAKING OF ULYSSES: (page 681) reviewed by H. G. PORTEUS. FREUD'S NEW LECTURES (page 683) reviewed by G. SCOTT MONCRIEFF. THE PHILOSOPHY OF COMMUNISM: (page 686) reviewed by THE REV. V. A. DEMANT. SAMUEL JOHNSON: (page 690) reviewed by WILLIAM KING. THE SEVENTEENTH CENTURY BACKGROUND: (page 692) reviewed by T. O. BEACHCROFT. DE BAUDELAIRE AU SURREALISME: (page 696) reviewed by PETER QUENNELL. SPENGLER AND OTHERS: (page 699) a review by A. W. G. RANDALL.

SHORTER NOTICES   FOREIGN PERIODICALS

PUBLISHED BY
FABER & FABER, LIMITED
24 RUSSELL SQUARE, LONDON, W.C.1
CONTINENTAL AGENTS: THE SERVIRE PRESS LTD., RIETZANGERLAAN 15, THE HAGUE, HOLLAND

Thirty Shillings per annum.

THE DUBLIN MAGAZINE

A Quarterly Review
of Literature, Science and Art.

Edited by SEUMAS O'SULLIVAN.

JULY—SEPTEMBER
1934.

Price 2/6

35   36

37. "Humanistic Quietism: A Foreword by Samuel Beckett." In *Collected Poems* by Thomas MacGreevy. Edited by Thomas Dillon Redshaw. [Dublin] New Writers' Press (1971). 8vo, original cloth, dust jacket.

Edition limited to 250 copies.
Reprint of *Poems* by Thomas MacGreevy (London, 1934), with the addition of five "fugitive pieces."

38. "A Case in a Thousand" [short story]. In *The Bookman*, Vol. LXXXVI, No. 515 (August 1934). Folio, original printed wrappers, uncut.

Inscribed at the beginning of Beckett's story: "For / John and Evelyn [Kobler] / with love from / Sam."
The issue contains, also, a less than laudatory article by Beckett on "Recent Irish Poetry," written under the pseudonym Andrew Belis. An autograph note, in Beckett's hand, on the front cover reads: "cf. pp. 235–244. AB was me." This article carries a second and similar presentation inscription in Beckett's hand.

39. "Ex Cathezra," review of *Make It New* by Ezra Pound; "Papini's Dante," review of *Dante Vivo* by Giovanni Papini; "The Essential and the Incidental," review of *Windfalls* by Sean O'Casey. In *The Bookman*, Vol. LXXXVII (Christmas 1934). Folio, original illustrated wrappers.

The first article is, at one and the same time, a thumping tribute to Pound and a tactful, subtle demonstration of the lamentable lapses in taste and judgment to which he was not infrequently disposed.

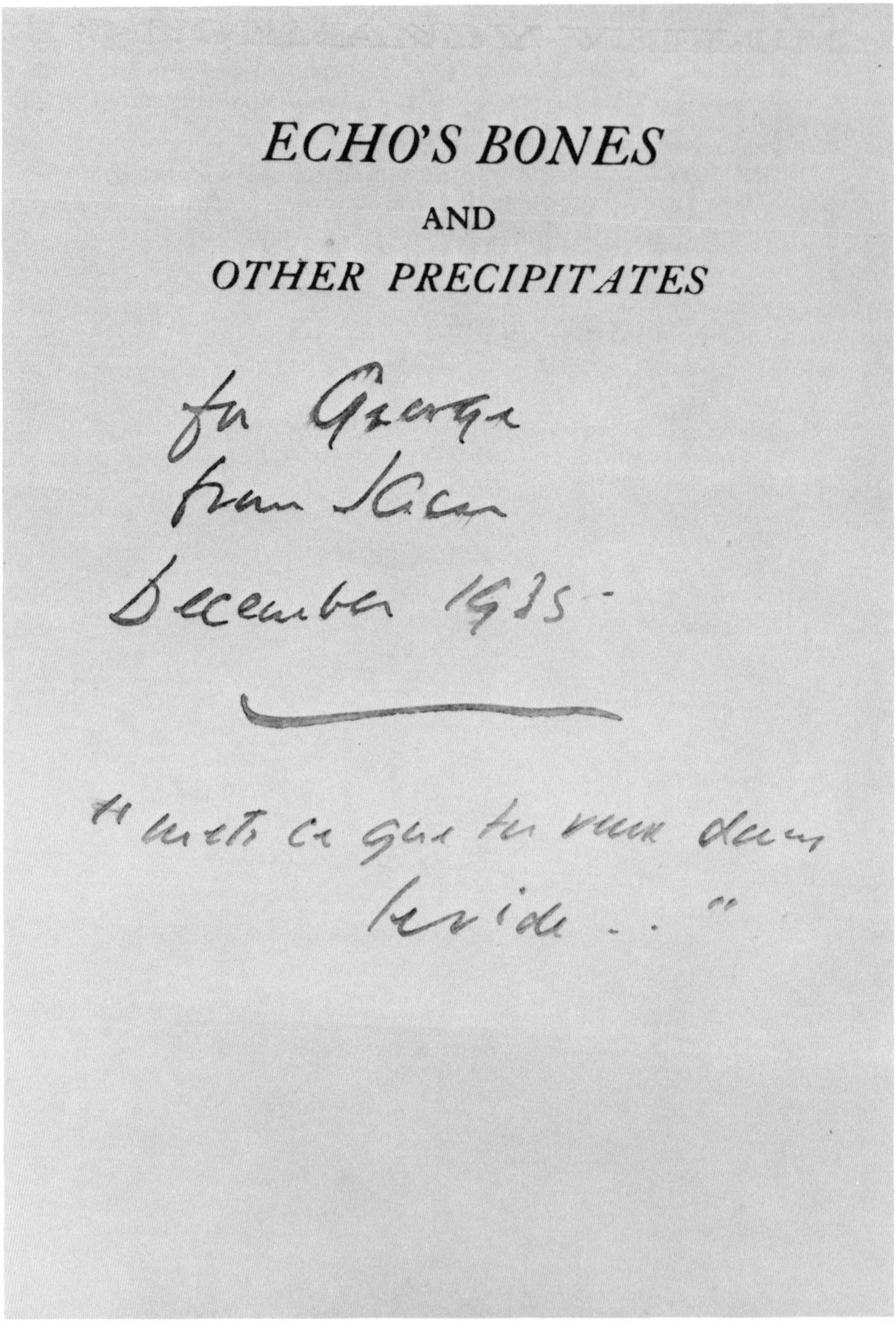

ECHO'S BONES

AND

OTHER PRECIPITATES

for George
from Sam
December 1935 –

"mets ce que tu veux dans
le vide . . "

41

ECHO'S BONES AND OTHER PRECIPITATES

Samuel Beckett met George Reavey, the future publisher of *Echo's Bones*, through Thomas MacGreevy at the end of 1928. Reavey had literary aspirations, an intimate knowledge of the Russian language and modern Russian literature, and an activist zeal in helping to promote the work of his friends. He was to be instrumental in placing *Murphy* with Routledge and, later, tireless in his efforts to find a taker for *Watt*. He worked out of a small literary agency called The European Literary Bureau and, along with it, juggled an even more modest publishing operation named Europa Press, which brought out, as one of its first books—at Beckett's expense—*Echo's Bones*. Reavey sold the literary agency before World War II but continued his efforts in Beckett's behalf in the immediate postwar years. In 1949 he moved to New York.

40. "Echo's Bones." Autograph manuscript, signed, 1 p., oblong 16mo.

The final poem in the collection published as *Echo's Bones and Other Precipitates.*

Fair copy, written out some years after publication. The poem had been submitted to *Poetry* magazine in 1934, along with three others. Of the four, three (this one, "Eneug I," and "Dortmunder") found their way into *Echo's Bones and Other Precipitates.*

41. *Echo's Bones and Other Precipitates.* Paris: Europa Press, 1935. Small 4to, original putty-colored printed wrappers, uncut.

The edition was limited to 327 copies of which 25 copies on Normandy Vellum were signed by the author. Two on this paper, marked A and B, were reserved for the author and the publisher. This is copy B, for George Reavey. It is inscribed on the half-title "for George / from Sam / December 1935 / — / 'mets ce que tu veux dans le vide . . .' "

An autograph note, in Reavey's hand, on the limitation page reads: ". . . This quotation in Sam's dedication is from a poem beginning 'Que m'importe l'aspect revêtu par le vide . . .' contained on page 19 of George Reavey's *Signes d'Adieu*, published by Europa Press, 1935. G.R."

There had apparently been some talk of giving the collection the title "Poems." In a card addressed to Reavey on 6 March 1935, Beckett wrote: "Not *Poems* after all, but: *Echo's Bones, and Other Precipitates.* C'est plus modeste."

On the other side of the card are the name and address of the sculptor Alberto Giacometti (in Giacometti's hand), raising at least the possibility that there may have been some thought of asking Giacometti to illustrate the book.

42. _____. Another copy, on Alfa paper, unnumbered, signed by Samuel Beckett on the title page.

Each poem is followed by an autograph note in Beckett's hand: e.g., after "The Vulture" Beckett has written "not without reference to / Goethe's / Dem Geier gleich, etc."; after "Alba," "39 Trinity College Dublin"; after "Dortmunder," "Cassel revisited"; after "Sanies I," "Exitus Redditus / this evening / Montparnasse / 1957"; after "Sanies II," "Ecole Normale / Paris 1929" and following the last poem in the book, "Echo's Bones," " 'Echo's Bones were turned / to stone.' / Ovid Metamorphoses?"

43. Documents relating to the publication and distribution of *Echo's Bones.*

(a) Typed letter, signed, from the printer, Guy Lévis Mano (Editions G.L.M.) to "Monsieur Reavey," 2 December 1935, sending his printing bill and asking for payment of the balance due "before the 15th of this month" (bill attached);

(b) printed subscription form;

(c) subscription list, in Reavey's hand, including, for the large-paper copies, the names of Beckett's friends Brian Coffey and Denis Devlin and Beckett's professor at Trinity, Rudmose-Brown, and for the regular issue, his mother and Sylvia Beach (two copies each); on the same sheet, a list of the review copies to be sent: Eliot, R[obert] Graves, Laura Riding, [I.A.?] Richards, Auden, and others, in addition to the expectable English and Irish reviews;

(d) duplicate of delivery form from G.L.M., 3 December 1935, for 75 copies including 25 on "*Japon*" [i.e., Normandy Vellum]; addressed to "M. Rivet" [French phonetic approximation of Reavey];

(e) autograph card, signed, "Tom" [MacGreevy] to Reavey, 30 December 1935: ". . . I want a couple of copies of Echo's Bones and wonder when I could come and get them. . .";

(f) autograph card, signed, Sylvia Beach to George Reavey, 17 January 1937: ". . . Can you please send me 2 copies of *Echo's Bones* by Beckett 'on sale'. . . ."

44. A representative selection of manuscripts, corrected typescripts, letters, and other documents exchanged between George Reavey and Deirdre Bair during the preparation of her biography of Samuel Beckett.

When Deirdre Bair was preparing her dissertation and the resulting *Samuel Beckett: A Biography*, she turned to Reavey, as one of Beckett's longtime friends, for guidance. He supplied her with background material, answered countless questions oral and written, oriented her on the ground and toward other knowledgeable sources, read and commented on her manuscript in its early stages and, during the course of a number of meetings in New York and at the Bair home in Connecticut, made himself available for consultation over a period of about four years while her dissertation and the book were in progress.

45. George Reavey. "Green and Blue," a poem dedicated, in Reavey's hand, "To Samuel Beckett." Typed manuscript, signed, 1 p., 4to.

With one variant from the version published in *Journal of Beckett Studies*, No. 2 (Summer 1977). (See below.)

46. "In Memoriam: George Reavey." In *Journal of Beckett Studies*, No. 2 (Summer 1977). 8vo, original wrappers, illustrated with a photograph by David Edwards of Ronald Pickup in Beckett's television play ". . . but the clouds. . . ."

Beckett's tribute to Reavey (1 May 1907–11 August 1976):

> Adieu George,
> to whom I owed so much, with whom shared
> so much, for whom cared so much

(Samuel Beckett, 5 February 1977).

It is preceded by two photographs of Reavey and is followed by a selection of Reavey's poems, including the one he dedicated to Beckett, entitled "Green and Blue."

The issue contains other tributes, by Julian Trevelyan, William Hayter, and Brian Coffey, and an interview with Reavey by James Knowlson concerning Beckett's early writing.

43c

47. Jean Reavey. "How It Is With Sam." Typed manuscript with autograph corrections, 4 pp., 4to.

George Reavey's wife tells the story, in abbreviated form, of the friendship of Beckett and her husband from the time "Thomas MacGreevy, later the director of the Dublin National Gallery [National Gallery of Ireland], brought George and Sam together sometime in 1929."

48. "George Reavey." From a drawing by A. Bilis done in Paris in 1931.

49. Snapshot taken by Peggy Guggenheim at her country place, Yew Tree Cottage, in Sussex, 1938. From left to right: Peggy's daughter, Pegeen, George Reavey, Geer van Velde, Gwynned Reavey, Samuel Beckett, Lisl van Velde.

50. Color photograph of Samuel Beckett taken in 1970 by Jean (Mrs. George) Reavey.

51. *Thorns of Thunder: Selected Poems by Paul Eluard.* With a drawing by Pablo Picasso. Edited by George Reavey. Translated from French by Samuel Beckett, Denis Devlin, David Gascoyne, Eugene Jolas, Man Ray, George Reavey, and Ruthven Todd. London: Europa Press & Stanley Nott [1936]. 8vo, original cloth, dust jacket.

One of 25 copies, of an edition of 600, reserved for the use of the author and publishers. This copy is designated I and carries Stanley Nott's name on the limitation page. It is inscribed on the half-title: "to Stanley Nott / Paul Eluard" and signed also by David Gascoyne, G. Reavey, and Ruthven Todd. Beneath these signatures is the inscription: "Samuel Beckett / Paris April 1972."
Beckett's contributions include "Lady Love," "The Invention," "Second Nature," "Scarcely Disfigured," "Scene," "Universe-Solitude," and "Out of Sight in the Direction of My Body." Most of the other translations had not been published before, but Beckett's had already appeared in the surrealist issue of *This Quarter* (1932). (See No. 23.)

52. Documents relating to *Thorns of Thunder.*

(a) Brian Coffey. Autograph letter to George Reavey concerning the translation of Eluard's poems from *Capitale de la douleur, L'Amour et la poésie* [sic], and *La Rose publique:* "Ask Beckett whether it would not be well to make the translations into a sequence of Eluard's work from the start [to] *Facile.* And to give his selection from the whole work, saying what poems he would like to translate. I'll make a selection from the whole work too—and [David] Gascoyne would do the same. Then we could examine the three selections and make a final choice." Apparently Coffey was scheduled to be one of the translators, but did not carry through.

(b) George Reavey. Carbon copy of typed letter, initialed, to *"Cher ami"* [Paul Eluard], 12 May 1936. As a result of a letter received from

49

48

PAUL ELUARD

THORNS
OF THUNDER

SELECTED POEMS

With a Drawing by Pablo Picasso

*

Edited by George Reavey

*

Translated from French by
Samuel Beckett, Denis Devlin, David
Gascoyne, Eugene Jolas, Man Ray,
George Reavey and Ruthven Todd

*

LONDON
EUROPA PRESS & STANLEY NOTT

51

Eluard "and other considerations," Reavey feels obliged to make changes in the original plan for the book. He will retain the title *Thorns of Thunder* but add *Selected Poems*. A reproduction of Picasso's drawing will be included in all copies, 50 of the regular issue will be signed, and there will be a unique copy with the original drawing (a portrait of Eluard) and the manuscript. He has arranged for Herbert Read to write a short preface. He has followed Eluard's recommendations for changing the order of the poems in *La Rose publique*. It won't be possible to put in "La Personnalité toujours neuve" because Gascoyne's version wasn't right. Reavey asked Beckett to make a different translation but he didn't have the time to do it on such short notice. Reavey is waiting for Max Ernst's design for the cover. He is hoping to arrange for an evening affair at which Eluard would read his poems and "some one of us" would read certain translations of them.

(c) Proof, in large format, of the drawing by Picasso (portrait of Eluard) used as the book's frontispiece.

(d) Proof of front flap of the dust jacket.

(e) Printed announcement: "In connection with the International Surrealist Exhibition . . . Friday, 26th June, at 9 p.m., Paul Eluard will recite his poems. English versions by Samuel Beckett, Denis Devlin, David Gascoyne, George Reavey."

(f) Poster for the International Surrealist Exhibition at the New Burlington Galleries, 12 June to 4 July. Admission 1/3.

(g) George Reavey. Typed manuscript with autograph corrections, 2 pp., 4to. Reavey's remarks introducing Eluard to his audience at the London reading: ". . . one of the few genuine lyrical poets writing in France, in Europe, at the present time. . . ."

(h) Paul Eluard. "L'Univers-Solitude." Autograph manuscript, 6 pp., 8vo. This poem, one of the longest in the collection, is from *La Vie immédiate*. It appears in *Thorns of Thunder* as translated by Samuel Beckett; however, Beckett translated only eleven of the sixteen sections in the French version as represented by this manuscript. The manuscript varies greatly from both the twenty-two-section version given in *La Vie immédiate* and from the text of an earlier appearance in the rare plaquette *A toute épreuve*.

(i) Paul Eluard. *A toute épreuve*. 24mo, original wrappers, uncut. Paris: Editions Surréalistes, 1930.

(j) Paul Eluard. Autograph letter, signed, to *"Mon cher Reavey,"* 1 September 1936. Eluard is on vacation with Picasso and other friends. Man Ray has just left. Eluard urges Reavey to send review copies of *Thorns of Thunder* to three friends in England and the United States.

(k) George Reavey. Carbon copy of typed letter to Stanley Nott, 14 June 1937. Reavey points out a discrepancy in Nott's statement of accounts for *Thorns of Thunder*; he plans to take over the stock of copies in Nott's possession.

52f.

52h.

53. "An Imaginative Work!" Review of *The Amaranthers* by Jack B. Yeats. In *The Dublin Magazine*, Vol. XI, No. 3, New Series (July–September 1936) [New York, 1967].

54. "Cascando." Carbon copy of typed manuscript, bearing the stamp of George Reavey's agency, "European Literary Bureau / 30 Red Lion Square London W.C.1," 1 p., 4to.

    Typed in the lower right corner: "(published in the Dublin Magazine Oct–Dec 1936.)"
    "Cascando" as it appears in this carbon typescript varies slightly from the version printed in *The Dublin Magazine*—most notably in the fact that here the poem is comprised of four sections whereas in *The Dublin Magazine* it has three. It differs substantively from the version printed in *Gedichte* and in later collections of Beckett's poems, where Beckett has added a new opening stanza of three lines in the first section.

55. "Cascando." In *The Dublin Magazine*, Vol. XI, No. 4, New Series (October–December 1936). Small 4to, full cloth, original printed wrappers bound in, uncut.

    Beckett later used the title of this poem for a radio play (1963), described under No. 299.

56. *Authors Take Sides on the Spanish War*. Published by *Left Review* [1937]. Crown 8vo, cloth, original printed wrappers bound in.

    The original broadside, headed "The Question," is tipped in. It was addressed to the "Writers and Poets of England, Scotland, Ireland and Wales" and asks: "Are you for, or against, the legal Government and the People of Republican Spain?" It was signed by Aragon, Auden, Nancy Cunard, Heinrich Mann, Pablo Neruda, Stephen Spender, Tristan Tzara, and five others and dated "Paris—June 1937."
    The writers addressed were asked for "a statement in not more than 6 lines." Some complied with, many exceeded, the limit. Beckett's statement was the briefest: "¡UPTHEREPUBLIC!"
    From the library of Evelyn Waugh, with Waugh's armorial bookplate.

56a. "The Question: Addressed to the Writers of Great Britain." Notebook compiled by Nancy Cunard and including the original maquette of the broadside, a proof of the broadside in its final form, and related documents, tipped in. Various formats, wrappers labeled in Nancy Cunard's hand "Spain / 1937." The hand-lettering, additions, and names of the signers are also in her hand.

    Other material tipped in includes thirteen letters from various writers—among them, Rebecca West, W. H. Auden, Rose Macaulay, and E. M. Forster—in reply to the questionnaire. These replies are the only survivors of the 150 to 200 received by Cunard. The remainder "disappeared during World War II, in my house at Réanville in Normandy."

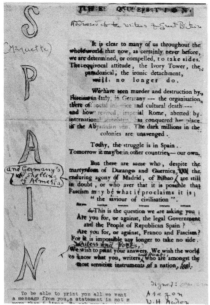
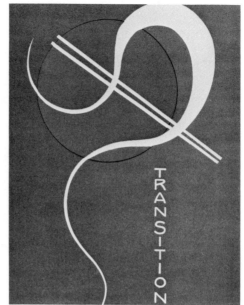

56a   57

Also included in the notebook are manuscripts and typescripts of seven poems printed in 1937 in a series of leaflets—"Los Poetas del Mundo Defienden al Pueblo Español"—"for distribution and sale in aid of funds for Republican Spain." The longest of these is Auden's four-page manuscript of his poem "Spain." It is accompanied by a cover letter from him to Nancy Cunard and the typescript from which the text was handset for No. V of "Los Poetas. . . ." Other contributions include a typed manuscript signed by Tristan Tzara—"Chant de Guerre Civile"—and works by Federico García Lorca, Pierre Robin, Langston Hughes, and Brian Howard.

57. "Ooftish." In *Transition* (tenth-anniversary issue), No. 27 (April–May 1938). Small 4to, original pictorial wrappers, from a design by Kandinsky.

Inscribed by Beckett: "for John and Evelyn [Kobler] / with love from Sam / Paris May 67."

The issue contains also Beckett's review and defense of Denis Devlin's *Intercessions*, published by George Reavey's Europa Press. Devlin was one of the small group of Irish writers Beckett had categorized, in his article "Recent Irish Poetry" (*The Bookman*, August 1934), as non-antiquarian: "aware of the vacuum which exists between perceiver and the thing perceived."

It was with this issue that the original and essential *Transition* ceased publication, a full eight years after the premature crepehanging. In reviewing its ten years of trailblazing activity in behalf of "a more imaginative concept of prose and poetry," of adhering to "a belief in the primacy of the creative spirit," Jolas cheerfully looked forward to seeking "a pan-symbolic, panlinguistic synthesis in the conception of a four-dimensional universe."

37

DERRIÈRE
LE MIROIR

GALERIE
MAEGHT

PIERRE
A FEU

Numéros 11 et 12   *Juin 1948*

BRAM et GEER van VELDE

ARTIST FRIENDS

Beckett's loyalty to his friends is legendary. In the case of artists whose work has touched him he has expressed his enthusiasm repeatedly and in a variety of manners. Which is only fitting, given the variety of tendencies represented by those artists: Jack B. Yeats, Bram and Geer van Velde, Henri Hayden, and Avigdor Arikha, for example.

58. "Hommage à Jack B. Yeats." Essays by Samuel Beckett, Pierre Schneider, and Jacques Putman. In *Les Lettres Nouvelles*, 2ᵉ année, No. 14 (April 1954). Crown 8vo, original printed wrappers. A review of an exhibition of Jack B. Yeats's paintings at the Paris Beaux-Arts gallery in March 1954.

59. "Geer van Velde." In *London Bulletin*, No. 2 (May 1938). Small 4to, original printed wrappers, uncut.

    George Reavey's copy, with his signature, of this review edited by the Belgian surrealist E.L.T. Mesens and devoted chiefly to the surrealist movement.
    Beckett writes "[Geer van Velde] believes painting should mind its own business, i.e. colour. *I.e.* no more say Picasso than Fabritius, Vermeer. Or inversely." On the verso of Beckett's page, his friends Brian Coffey and George Reavey also pay tribute to Geer van Velde.

60. "La Peinture des van Velde ou le monde et le pantalon." In *Cahiers d'Art*, 20ᵉ–21ᵉ années (1945–46). Folio, original printed wrappers.

    At the end of World War II, while he was at St.-Lô, Beckett was commissioned by *Cahiers d'Art* to write an article on the painting of Abraham (later Bram) and Geer van Velde. The subtitle is derived from the joke Beckett uses at the beginning of his essay: a tailor justifies his slowness in getting a pair of trousers made—impeccably, is the implication—by referring to the state of the world, created in only six days. The story reappears in *Fin de partie (Endgame)*.
    Beckett's article is a greatly underrated piece of art criticism, of a kind few Frenchmen would be capable of turning out. It is plain talk, straight from the shoulder, at moments subtle to the point of near-obscurity but marked throughout by a sense of humor—and of reality—which the great embroiderers of the art jargon, *à la manière de Malraux*, would neither aspire to nor, in many cases, understand. It closes on an ironic note which might be applied to the early reception of Beckett's own work:

    > Que deviendra, dans cette foire, cette peinture solitaire, solitaire de la solitude qui se couvre la tête, de la solitude qui tend les bras.

Cette peinture dont la moindre parcelle contient plus d'humanité vraie que toutes leurs processions vers un bonheur de mouton sacré.

Je suppose qu'elle sera lapidée.

61. "Bram et Geer van Velde. Peintres de l'empêchement." In *Derrière le Miroir*, Nos. 11 et 12. [Editions] Pierre à Feu. [Paris] Galerie Maeght, June 1948. Folio, loose in sheets, uncut.

    This witty essay on the van Velde brothers is written in the classic style of the Beckett trilogy (*Malone Meurt*, for example, with the composition of which it is roughly contemporaneous).

62. "Three Dialogues." In *Transition Forty-Nine*, No. 5. Paris: Transition Press, 1949. 12mo, original illustrated wrappers with a cover design by Matisse, uncut.

    Conversations between Beckett and Matisse's son-in-law, the art historian Georges Duthuit, on Tal Coat, André Masson, and Bram van Velde. The article is followed by a text, "Some Sayings of Bram van Velde," translated by Beckett, but printed unsigned.
    Inscribed at the head of the article: "for John and Evelyn [Kobler] with / love from Sam / Paris May 67."

63. "Dialogue Samuel Beckett—Georges Duthuit." Beckett's translation into French of the third dialogue in the series printed in *Transition Forty-Nine*—the one concerned with Bram van Velde. [Paris] 1957. Folio, sheet folded in the middle.

    This broadside was issued in conjunction with an exhibition of Bram van Velde's work held at the Galerie Michel Warren from 7 May to 1 June 1957.
    Inscribed "Dear Jake Schwartz / thought you might like to have this / Sam Beckett / Paris May 1957."

64. *Bram van Velde* [essays by Samuel Beckett, Georges Duthuit, and Jacques Putman]. With twelve color reproductions of Bram van Velde's work. [Paris: Le Musée de Poche, 1958]. 12mo, original pictorial wrappers.

    Two of the four essays in this edition are by Beckett. The first is a short extract taken from his article "Bram et Geer van Velde. Peintres de l'empêchement," which appeared in *Derrière le Miroir* in 1948. The second text is a long extract from Beckett's translation of "Three Dialogues," which was first printed in *Transition Forty-Nine*, No. 5, in 1949.

65. "Bram van Velde." In *Bram van Velde* by Samuel Beckett, Georges Duthuit, Jacques Putman. Translated from the French by Olive Classe and Samuel Beckett. With photographs in black and white and in color and with twelve tipped-in color plates. New York: Grove Press (1960). 12mo, original pictorial wrappers, uncut.

Inscribed on the half-title: "for John and Evelyn [Kobler] / affectionately from Sam / Ussy April 69."

66. *Bram van Velde*. With texts by Samuel Beckett, Jacques Putman, and Georges Duthuit. With tipped-in color plates and other illustrations and a catalogue of the work. Torino and Paris: Fratelli Pozzo and Guy Le Prat [1961]. Oblong folio, original cloth, pictorial dust jacket. One of 1,500 numbered copies for France.

67. *Proust* and *Three Dialogues*. London: John Calder (1965). 12mo, original leather-backed cloth, all edges gilt.

   One of 100 numbered copies signed by Beckett and specially bound.
   Inscribed on the title page: "For / John and Evelyn [Kobler] / with love from Sam / Paris June 1971."

68. "Textes Critiques" [two by Samuel Beckett]. In *Bram van Velde. Edité à l'occasion de la rétrospective Bram van Velde*. With illustrations in black and white and in color. Paris: Musée National d'Art Moderne [1970]. Small 4to, original decorative wrappers.

69. "Henri Hayden." In *Henri Hayden. Recent Paintings*. London: The Waddington Galleries, 1959. 8vo, original blue wrappers, uncut.

   Hayden and Beckett met and became good friends during their stay in the town of Roussillon, in the Vaucluse, during the German occupation of France.

70. "Pas trace de surenchère . . ." and two other short texts on Henri Hayden. In *Hayden: Soixante ans de peinture 1908–1968*. [Paris] Musée National d'Art Moderne, 1968. Sq. 12mo, original illustrated wrappers.

   The photographic portrait which serves as frontispiece is signed in ink "H. Hayden" and Beckett has written a presentation inscription above his texts: "for John [Kobler] from Sam / Paris February / 1970."

70

71. "bon bon il est un pays." In *Avigdor Arikha: Paintings, Gouaches, Drawings*. London: The Matthiesen Gallery, 8 April to 2 May 1959. Small 4to, original pictorial wrappers.

This is the poem "Accul," which originally appeared in *Les Cahiers des Saisons*, No . 2 (October 1955). It was printed also in *Gedichte* (Limes Verlag, 1959) and in *Poèmes* (Editions de Minuit, 1968).

72. "Pour Avigdor Arikha." In *Avigdor Arikha: Dessins 1965–1970*. Paris: Centre National d'Art Contemporain [1970]. Oblong 8vo, original illustrated wrappers.

Inscribed on the series title page: "For Evelyn and John [Kobler] / with affection from / Avigdor."
Published in conjunction with an exhibition of Arikha's work at the Centre National d'Art Contemporain from 8 December 1970 to 18 January 1971. Text by Barbara Rose. The catalogue contains two portraits of Beckett by Arikha.

73. *Avigdor Arikha. Drawings 1965/66*. With a text by Samuel Beckett: "For Avigdor Arikha." Jerusalem and Tel-Aviv: Tarshish Books and Dvir. Folio, original linen-backed decorative boards, in publisher's cloth slipcase.

Inscribed to John and Evelyn Kobler by Arikha.
One of the plates is a silverpoint portrait of Samuel Beckett.

74. *Carte-postale* photograph showing Geer van Velde and his wife Lisl.

MURPHY

Murphy, Beckett's great first published novel, was rejected by more than forty publishers, among them the august Boston firm of Houghton Mifflin, whose editorial pasha was Ferris Greenslet, a man of legendary if somewhat eccentric editorial style. He was renowned for his manner of reading a manuscript: what he called "pricking it to see if it bled." He would dig into it with his letter opener three times, in that manner selecting three pages at random. If those three didn't interest him, the manuscript went back where it came from. Apparently when he dug into *Murphy*, *Murphy* bit back. After an interminable delay, Houghton Mifflin recommended that Beckett cut the novel by one third. They didn't care much for the title, either. A propos of their report, Beckett wrote to Mary Manning Howe on 14 November 1936:

> Reavey wrote enclosing a letter from Greensletandhindrance. I am exhorted to ablate 33.3 recurring to all eternity of my work. I have thought of a better plan. Take every 500th word, punctuate carefully and publish a poem in prose in the Paris Daily Mail. Then the rest separately and privately, with a forewarning from Geoffrey [Thompson], as the ravings of a schizoid, or serially, in translation, in the Zeitschrift für Kitsch. My next work shall be on rice paper wound about a spool, with a perforated line every six inches and on sale in Boots. The length of each chapter will be carefully calculated to suit with the average free motion. And with every copy a free sample of some laxative to promote sales. The Beckett Bowel Books, Jesus in farto. Issued in imperishable tissue. Thistledown end papers. All edges disinfected. 1000 wipes of clean fun. Also in Braille for anal pruritics. All Sturm and no Drang.

Along the route, *Murphy* did occasionally find a sympathetic reader. Acting as Beckett's agent, George Reavey sent the typescript to J. M. Dent & Sons, where it was read by the writer Richard Church, a more sensitive judge of literary values than the average publisher's editor. Church wrote to Reavey:

> I think this man is a most remarkable and highly equipped writer. The humour, the sophistication, the sense of structure, and the queer originality make me agree with you that he is a man fully worth while fostering. I have been on the telephone with Harold Raymond of Chatto & Windus and said what I think about the book and also that I believe they are making a mistake if they let him go. Raymond has accordingly asked to see the manuscript again and I am taking the liberty of sending it to him but he does not want Beckett to know this in case he has to come to the same conclusion as the other directors and again disappoint the author.

Whether Mr. Raymond turned thumbs down or the sales record of *More*

Pricks Than Kicks proved an insurmountable barrier to acceptance, Chatto and Windus abstained.

Finally, *Murphy* was accepted by Routledge on the recommendation of Herbert Read, a man of taste in art and literature. The English reviewers were of a different stripe, however. In a letter written on stationery from the Café du Dôme, Beckett wrote to Arland Ussher on 27 March 1938: "The critics have all betrayed the same annoyance. Like the dog's hindquarters when the spine is touched in the right place."

At the end of World War II, when Beckett passed through London en route to Dublin, he discovered that of the 1,500 copies printed, Routledge had sold only 618 and remaindered the rest—without consulting him, of course. For his years of anguish over *Murphy* Beckett received "in all £20 ([minus] income tax)," he wrote to George Reavey on 15 December 1946.

75. "Murphy." Carbon copy of typed manuscript, signed, 26 June 1936 [date of completion], 192 pp., folio, cloth-backed buff wrappers.

This copy of the typescript contains some deletions, emendations, and annotations. The cover is marked in Beckett's hand, in blue crayon, "Murphy / Samuel Beckett," and in ink, "Original typescript / of *Murphy* / written in London / and Dublin." The last page (unnumbered) bears the date and Beckett's address: "Samuel Beckett / 6 Clare Street / Dublin / Irish Free State."

76. *Murphy.* London: George Routledge & Sons (1938). 12mo, original cloth.

First edition. With the publisher's original blurb and order form.
Inscribed on the title page: "For John & Evelyn [Kobler] / with love from Sam / Paris June 1971."

77. *Murphy.* New York: Grove Press [1957]. 12mo, original linen-backed boards. Second edition. One of 100 numbered and specially bound copies, signed by Beckett.

78. *Murphy.* London: John Calder (1963). 12mo, original wrappers, illustrated with a photograph of Beckett. Third edition.

79. *Murphy.* Paris: Bordas, 1947. 8vo, original printed wrappers, uncut and unopened.

First edition, in the original wrappers, of Beckett's translation of *Murphy* into French. No large-paper copies were printed.
The translation is dedicated to Beckett's friend Alfred Péron, whom he had met when Péron came to Trinity College Dublin as an exchange lecturer in French.
This copy is inscribed by Beckett on the title page: "for John [Kobler] / affectionately / Sam / Paris April 1966."
On 15 December 1945 Beckett wrote to Reavey, "Since my last

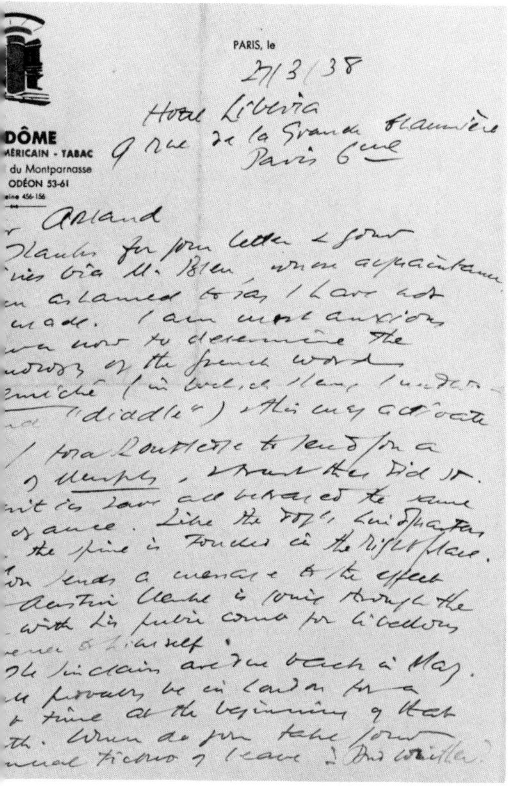

Handwritten letter (top left):

PARIS, le

27/3/38

Hôtel Libéria
9 rue de la Grande Chaumière
Paris 6e

DÔME
MÉRICAIN - TABAC
du Montparnasse
ODÉON 53-61
...456-156

Arland

Thanks for your letter & for [illegible] via Mr Blen, whose acquaintance I am ashamed to say I have not made. I am most anxious now to determine the source of the French word [illegible] (in which Henry [illegible] ["diddle"]) & [illegible] activate [illegible] Routledge to send for a [illegible] of Murphy, [illegible] they did it. [illegible] Like the Top, his [illegible] the [illegible] is [illegible] in the right place. [illegible] sends a message to the effect [illegible] Austin Clarke is [illegible] through the [illegible] with his public come for [illegible] [illegible] & himself. The Sinclairs are due back in May, [illegible] probably be in London for a [illegible] time at the beginning of that [illegible]. When do you take your annual fiction of leave? Bon travailler.

Typescript page (page 8 of Murphy):

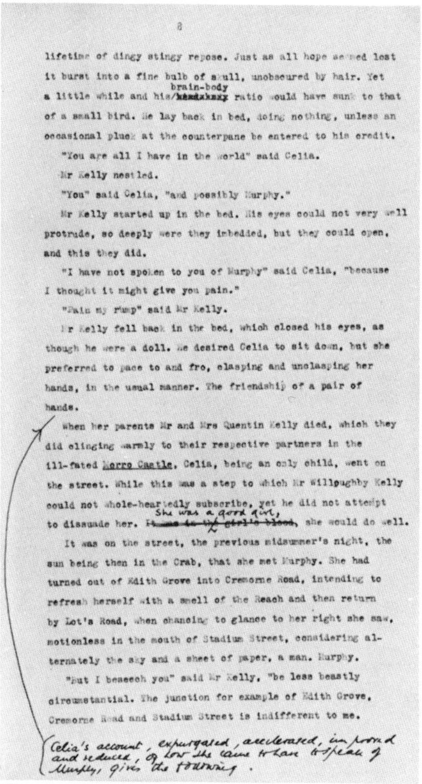

8

lifetime of dingy stingy repose. Just as all hope seemed lost it burst into a fine bulb of skull, unobscured by hair. Yet a little while and his/handsksxy brain-body ratio would have sunk to that of a small bird. He lay back in bed, doing nothing, unless an occasional pluck at the counterpane be entered to his credit.

"You are all I have in the world" said Celia.

Mr Kelly nestled.

"You" said Celia, "and possibly Murphy."

Mr Kelly started up in the bed. His eyes could not very well protrude, so deeply were they imbedded, but they could open, and this they did.

"I have not spoken to you of Murphy" said Celia, "because I thought it might give you pain."

"Pain my rump" said Mr Kelly.

Mr Kelly fell back in the bed, which closed his eyes, as though he were a doll. He desired Celia to sit down, but she preferred to pace to and fro, clasping and unclasping her hands, in the usual manner. The friendship of a pair of hands.

When her parents Mr and Mrs Quentin Kelly died, which they did clinging warmly to their respective partners in the ill-fated Morro Castle, Celia, being an only child, went on the street. While this was a step to which Mr Willoughby Kelly could not whole-heartedly subscribe, yet he did not attempt to dissuade her. She was a good girl, she would do well.

It was on the street, the previous midsummer's night, the sun being then in the Crab, that she met Murphy. She had turned out of Edith Grove into Cremorne Road, intending to refresh herself with a smell of the Reach and then return by Lot's Road, when chancing to glance to her right she saw, motionless in the mouth of Stadium Street, considering alternately the sky and a sheet of paper, a man. Murphy.

"But I beseech you" said Mr Kelly, "be less beastly circumstantial. The junction for example of Edith Grove, Cremorne Road and Stadium Street is indifferent to me.

Celia's account, expurgated, accelerated, improved and reduced, of how she came to have to speak of Murphy, gives the following.

See page 43   75

76

Book jacket flap:

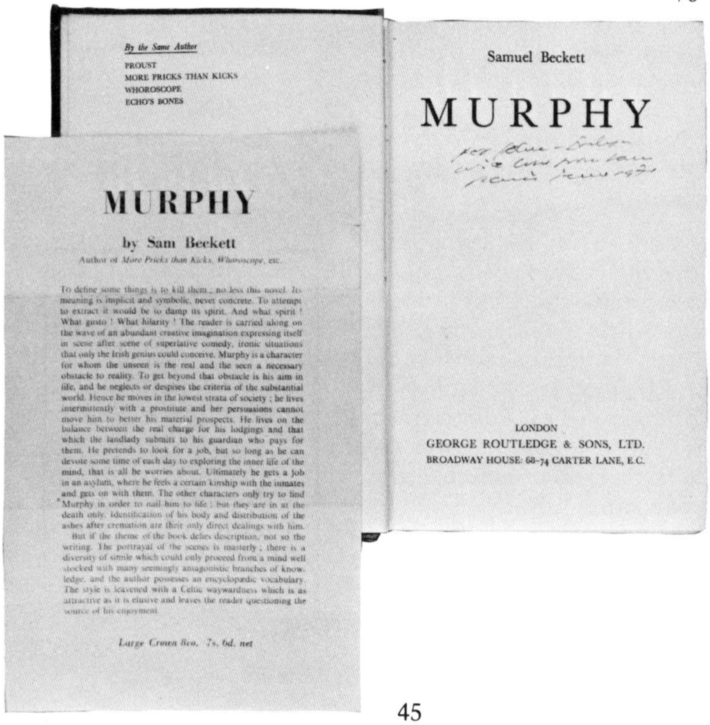

By the Same Author
PROUST
MORE PRICKS THAN KICKS
WHOROSCOPE
ECHO'S BONES

MURPHY
by Sam Beckett
Author of More Pricks than Kicks, Whoroscope, etc.

To define some things is to kill them; no less this novel. Its meaning is implicit and symbolic, never concrete. To attempt to extract it would be to dump its spirit. And what spirit! What gusto! What hilarity! The reader is carried along on the wave of an abundant creative imagination expressing itself in scene after scene of superlative comedy, ironic situations that only the Irish genius could conceive. Murphy is a character for whom the unseen is the real and the seen a necessary obstacle to reality. To get beyond that obstacle is his aim in life, and he neglects or despises the criteria of the substantial world. Hence he moves in the lowest strata of society; he lives intermittently with a prostitute and her persuasions cannot move him to better his material prospects. He lives on the balance between the real charge for his lodgings and that which the landlady submits to his guardian who pays for them. He pretends to look for a job, but so long as he can devote some time of each day to exploring the inner life of the mind, that is all he worries about. Ultimately he gets a job in an asylum, where he feels a certain kinship with the inmates and gets on with them. The other characters only try to find Murphy in order to nail him to life; but they are in at the death only. Identification of his body and distribution of the ashes after cremation are their only direct dealings with him.

But if the theme of the book defies description, not so the writing. The portrayal of the scenes is masterly; there is a diversity of simile which could only proceed from a mind well stocked with many seemingly antagonistic branches of knowledge, and the author possesses an encyclopaedic vocabulary. The style is leavened with a Celtic waywardness which is as attractive as it is elusive and leaves the reader questioning the source of his enjoyment.

Large Crown 8vo. 7s. 6d. net

Title page:

Samuel Beckett

MURPHY

[handwritten inscription, illegible]

LONDON
GEORGE ROUTLEDGE & SONS, LTD.
BROADWAY HOUSE: 68-74 CARTER LANE, E.C.

45

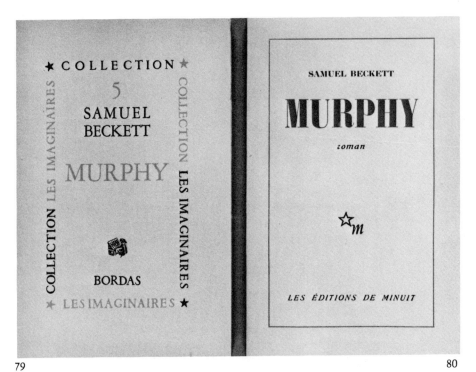

letter to you my position has been considerably simplified. I have signed a contract with the Editions . . . Bordas for all future work in French and English (including translations) and my affairs are now entirely in their hands. . . . They are publishing in the first place my French translation of *Murphy* and have already paid me handsomely enough (to one used to British generosity) both for my translation and an advance on royalties."

80. *Murphy.* Paris: Bordas, 1947. 8vo, original first-edition sheets from Bordas bound by Les Editions de Minuit in their own wrappers, uncut and unopened.

Beckett's optimism about his future with Bordas didn't survive the launching of the French edition of *Murphy*. Beckett couldn't accept the happy-marionnette role that publishers' publicity departments try to cajole authors into playing, and in spite of some good reviews, the book failed to catch on. Published in Bordas's series "Les Imaginaires" in an edition of 3,000 copies, *Murphy* languished in its bins. By the time Jérôme Lindon of Les Editions de Minuit took over as Beckett's publisher, four years later, fewer than 100 copies had been sold. The remaining copies and unbound sheets were bound in the characteristic Minuit wrappers.

This copy is inscribed on the title page: "This is original edition / of my translation of / *Murphy* / For Jake Schwartz / Sam. Beckett."

81. Brian Coffey. "Murphy." Typed manuscript, initialed, Paris, March 1938, 3 pp., 4to.

A review (unpublished?) by one of Beckett's friends.

". . . this time no venetian hair of tempered glass sliding into the sacred fount but the gash of the dirk, the hard new style."

82. Richard Church. Typed letter, signed, to George Reavey, 12 January 1937. On the letterhead of J. M. Dent & Sons, Publishers.

Delighted by his reading of the typescript of *Murphy*, Church has urged Chatto & Windus to continue publishing Beckett.

83. Margaret Frohnknecht. Typed letter, signed, to Samuel Beckett, 22 February 1938.

Mrs. Frohnknecht had learned from her cousin Helen Joyce and Helen's husband, Giorgio, that Beckett "had written a book of which they and Mr. Joyce senior thought very highly." As a manuscript reader for Random House and Harcourt Brace, she offers "to read the manuscript [*Murphy*] and pass it on to either one of them."

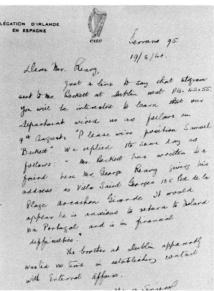

82   84

84. P. J. O'Byrne. Autograph letter, signed, to George Reavey, on the letterhead of the Irish Legation in Serrano, Spain, 19 August 1940.

While France was preparing, in the fall of 1939, for the inevitable German invasion, Beckett decided that, rather than flee, he wanted to stay in Paris, where he was determinedly translating *Murphy* into French. But to do so, he needed papers verifying that he was a "neutral alien." He applied for the necessary papers in early September, but the bureaucracy—now overtaxed because of the war—was especially slow. He wrote to Reavey on 26 September, "I have no news of my application & God knows when I shall. I am thinking of going to see [Constantine] Cremin at the Irish Legation, though I don't suppose he can do anything." Beckett's supposition proved true. Two months later he wrote to Reavey, "I have had no news of my *démarche*," and again in May 1940, "I never had a reply to the application I made in September. I have offered myself now to drive an ambulance. If they take me, they will take me soon."

Having no papers and no money, Beckett was finally forced to leave just ahead of the German occupation of Paris, and he headed for Vichy, where Joyce was. From there, by train and bus and on foot, he reached Arcachon. He wrote to Reavey, then in Madrid, that he would like to get back to Ireland. Reavey so informed the Irish Legation in Madrid and waited for Beckett to appear. According to this letter from Mr. O'Byrne to Reavey, Beckett was trying to reach Ireland via Portugal. Bureaucratic delays once more disrupted his plans, but this time they worked in his favor: he was able to return to Paris, where he stayed until October 1942.

ENGLISH TO FRENCH

Beckett saw fit not to leave France during the Nazi occupation. He served the Resistance quietly and effectively, both in Paris and in the Vaucluse. At the end of the war he was awarded the *Croix de Guerre* with gold star (as well as the *Médaille de la Résistance*), but didn't tell his friends about it.

During those years, Beckett was working on a second novel, *Watt*, which, like *Murphy*, he wrote in English. He translated *Murphy* into French, worked on *Mercier et Camier*, a French novel which he withheld from publication for many years, and on his French play *Eleuthéria*.

Beckett's colleague at the Ecole Normale Supérieure, Jean Thomas, had recognized in Beckett a poet-in-embryo, but he had no indication, he has recalled, that he was dealing with a future French writer. That kind of transformation, to a Frenchman more than to most, is a puzzling phenomenon. Frenchmen traditionally have found it normal that everyone else should speak French; for one thing, that saves them the trouble of learning anyone else's language. But that any outlander should use their language as effectively as Beckett did in his great trilogy—*Molloy*, *Malone Meurt (Malone Dies)*, and *L'Innommable (The Unnamable)*—and in *Godot* is, or at least was, unthinkable. For a writer in middle years, with a mastery of his style, to change from one language to another is a courageous, an intrepid but, potentially, a foolhardy act.

What brought him to it? It had long since become clear that France was his spiritual home. His education, his lectureship at the Ecole Normale Supérieure, his frequent returning to Paris in the course of throwing off a smothering family environment all point in that direction. Picasso, threatened by his own virtuosity and burdened by the weight of tradition, recreated form to shape a new imagery. And so it was with Beckett. He, too, had oppressive traditions to escape from, chief among them what he has called the "Anglo-Irish exuberance and automatisms."

Associated with that was another urgent need: to find his true subject. Like Saul on the road to Damascus, like Paul Valéry during his *nuit de Gênes*, Beckett had his blinding revelation one stormy postwar night as he wandered around the Dublin harbor area. He suddenly realized he had one subject—himself—and henceforward he would tell that story, with all its dark side, directly, through a narrator whose voice would always be his own. What he had recorded over the years, he would now play back. That revelation is reflected in an early draft version of *Krapp's Last Tape* in HRC's Beckett collection:

> Intellectually a year of profound gloom until that wonderful night in March, at the end of the pier, in the high wind, when suddenly I saw the whole thing. The turning-point, at last. This, I imagine, is what I have chiefly to set down this evening, against the day when my work will be done and perhaps no place in my memory, and no thankfulness, for the miracle—(*pause*)—for the fire that set it

alight. What I saw was that the assumption I had been going on all my life, namely—*(He switches off machine impatiently, winds tape forward, switches on again)*—granite rocks the foam flying up in the light of the beacon and the anemometer spinning like a propellor, clear to me at last that the dark I have struggled to keep
      at bay
~~out of my work~~ is in reality my most valuable—*(He curses, switches off, winds tape forward, switches on again)*—strange association till my dying day of storm and night with the light of understanding and the—*(He curses louder, switches off, winds tape forward, switches on again)* . . .

In making that change of subject, of tone, in letting "the dark" *into* his work, Beckett changed languages. He needed to cut away the excess, to strip away the color, to tell his story simply and directly. French, he has said, gave him distance from the writing and enabled him to assess it more clearly. It slowed down the whole process of formulation for him. If he was to impoverish form in keeping with the revelation of his proper subject-matter and his espousal of mental poverty, then French was the keener cutting-edge. He had tried it earlier with the poems and *nouvelles*, but the definite switch came after his return to Dublin in the summer of 1945 when he began work on *Molloy*. English had now grown to be the foreign language, so to remain for ten years.

ELEUTHÉRIA

"Eleuthéria"—the title is the Greek word for freedom—is Beckett's first play. It was written in French and is still unpublished, by his wish, even though it had been announced for forthcoming publication, along with *L'Innommable* and *En attendant Godot*, in both *Molloy* and *Malone Meurt*.

Beckett had already begun to write in French—the poems and early stories and, beginning in July 1946, *Mercier et Camier*. But although "Eleuthéria" was written in French and followed those earlier works, it is still very closely related, in tone and spirit, to even earlier things that he had written in English. In that sense it is a late-blooming transitional work and, even though preceded by other works in French, forms a bridge between Beckett the English-language writer and Beckett the French writer.

Jean Vilar was interested in "Eleuthéria" for the Théâtre National Populaire and asked that Beckett compress it into one act, but Beckett wasn't willing to comply.

85. "Eleuthéria." Autograph manuscript, signed, 1947, 203 pp. in two notebooks, small 4to.

   With revisions, deletions, and additions throughout, in blue ink and in pencil. Both notebooks contain doodles and several pages of diagrams relating to the stage sets and the characters' positions on stage.
   The first notebook—an exercise book with purple wrappers—contains "Acte I," begun on 18 January 1947. The front cover has, in addition to the title, Beckett's signature and the autograph note: "Prior to Godot, 1947. / Unpublished, / jettisoned." The final three pages (plus two pages of revision) provide both an explanation of the parallel action which is to take place during Acts I and II, on a split stage, and a synopsis of each of the three acts.
   The second notebook—an exercise book with blue wrappers—contains "Actes II et III," and is signed by Beckett. The final page of the text gives the date of completion as 24 February 1947. The "curious material . . . much of which is illegible" (in the last three pages of the notebook) referred to in Admussen, *The Samuel Beckett Manuscripts. A Study* (Boston: G. K. Hall & Co., 1979), p. 106, consists of drafts, in variant forms, of Beckett's poem "Accul" (see Nos. 71, 248).

86. "Eleuthéria. Pièce en 3 Actes." Photocopy of typed manuscript, 135 pp., 4to.

   With substantive variants from the autograph manuscript. An autograph note on the title page reads: "Written 1946? / Never attempted English translation. / This is photo of my original typescript / presumably now with Grove Press or / Editions de Minuit. / No idea who has original MS. / Never edition of any kind if I / can help it. / Samuel Beckett / Paris / March 69."

This copy of the "original typescript" has an expanded version of the autograph notes on the play's parallel action, entitled here, "Note sur la Disposition de la Scène et l'Action Marginale." Unlike the autograph manuscript, the typescript includes a listing of the characters (17 in all) and gives the setting as Paris and the time as three consecutive winter afternoons.

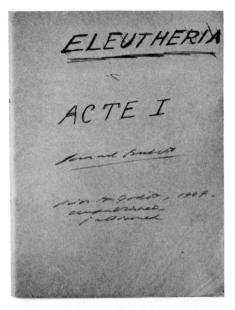

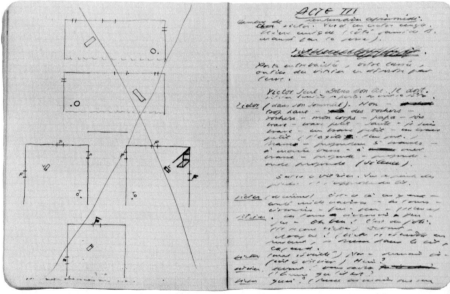

85

THE TRILOGY:
MOLLOY, MALONE MEURT, L'INNOMMABLE
MOLLOY, MALONE DIES, THE UNNAMABLE

The exact chronology of Beckett's immediate postwar writings is less than clear, but the five-year period that followed the war was one of intense and sustained creative activity. The trilogy—Beckett's three major novels—was written during those years and although the Texas manuscript of *Molloy* shows a starting date of 2 May 1947, Beckett has said that he actually began working on *Molloy* in the summer of 1945. All three novels were written rapidly: six months, six months, and nine months, respectively. Beckett's switch from English to French, which became operative at that time, had not slowed him down. *Au contraire.*

On 8 July 1948, Beckett wrote to George Reavey: "I am now retyping, for rejection by the publishers, *Malone Meurt*, the last I hope of the series Murphy, Watt, Mercier & Camier, Molloy, not to mention the 4 Nouvelles & Eleuthéria. . . ." At that time, Beckett had had a nibble from "a young publisher . . . I forget his name, Editions K I think." K's interest waned, as did the interest of at least five others who followed. Meanwhile Beckett continued to translate portions of *Molloy* and *Malone Meurt* into English and finished typing *L'Innommable*.

In the fall of 1950, through a series of those fortuitous encounters that André Breton, drawing on Engels, Lautréamont, and Freud, labeled *le hasard objectif*, the paths of Beckett's manuscripts and of Jérôme Lindon, the new publisher of a small and all-but-bankrupt Paris publishing house, Les Editions de Minuit, converged, for the greater glory of all concerned. Enchanted from the opening lines by what he has referred to as the "overwhelming beauty" of the text of *Molloy*, Lindon signed a contract which committed him to publish all three of the novels "as quickly as possible." In return, he paid Samuel Beckett a "generous advance" (S. B. *dixit*) amounting to about $70. About a month later, on 11 December 1950, Beckett wrote to Reavey: "I have signed a contract with the Editions of Minuit for all work. They contract specifically for the three 'novels' already written. The first, *Molloy*, should be out in January. Bordas, on the brink of bankruptcy (not *entirely* my fault), have released me."

87. "Molloy." Autograph manuscript, 2 May 1947–1 November 1947, 602 pp., small 4to.

> This, the original manuscript, was written in four notebooks, three of them cloth-backed, one spiral-bound. With some corrections and additions and occasional doodles and word counts, but giving evidence of having been written rapidly and with fewer hesitations and *repentirs*

than *Watt*, for example. Marked at periodic intervals with place and date of composition, from Foxrock, Paris, and (mostly) Menton, frequently on a day-to-day basis. The opening passage of *Molloy* was added at the beginning after the rest had been completed.

The second notebook contains diagrams and calculations concerning the celebrated passage about Molloy's manipulation of the sixteen sucking stones from one pocket to another. The last page has biographical notes in Beckett's hand. The previous two pages have diagrams and schemes for crossword puzzles in an unidentified hand.

88. *Molloy*. Paris: Les Editions de Minuit (1951). 8vo, original printed wrappers, uncut and unopened.

First edition, one of 50 numbered large-paper copies on *vélin supérieur Albelio*. Signed by Beckett on the title page.

89. *Molloy*. [Paris] Les Editions de Minuit (1951). 8vo, original printed wrappers, uncut and unopened.

This copy of the first edition, signed by Beckett on the flyleaf, is one of 500 numbered copies on *papier Alfa* printed for "Les Amis des Editions de Minuit."

90. "Two Fragments." In *Transition Fifty*, No. 6. Paris: Transition Press, 1950. 12mo, original illustrated wrappers, uncut.

The first fragment is an extract from *Molloy*; the second, from *Malone Meurt*. Both were translated by Beckett. These English translations were published before any part of the original French versions.

This issue of *Transition* contains, as well, two unsigned translations by Beckett: the last chapter of *Armand*, by Emmanuel Bove, and "Zone," a poem by Guillaume Apollinaire, from his collection *Alcools* (see No. 370).

91. "Extract from *Molloy*." Translated from the French by P. W. Bowles. In *Merlin*, Vol. II, No. 2 (Autumn 1953). Crown 8vo, original printed wrappers, uncut. Signed by Beckett, above the title. With a drawing by Robert Culff.

92. "Extract from *Molloy*." In *The Paris Review*, No. 5 (Spring 1954). 8vo, original illustrated wrappers, uncut.

This extract is the hilarious passage about Molloy's sixteen sucking stones. It was later reprinted as "Stones" in *Best Short Stories from The Paris Review*, edited by William Styron (New York, 1959).

93. "Molloy" [extract]. In *New World Writing*, Vol. V [April 1954]. 12mo, original printed wrappers.

Inscribed by Beckett: "for John & Evelyn [Kobler] / affectionately / Sam / May 1967."

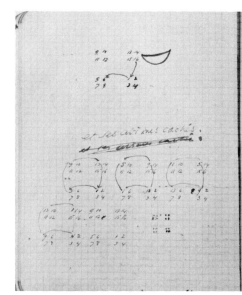

87

DU MEME AUTEUR

———

A paraître chez le même éditeur :

MALONE MEURT (roman)

L'INNOMMABLE (roman)

ELEUTHERIA (pièce en 3 actes)

EN ATTENDANT GODOT (pièce en 2 actes)

Aux Editions Bordas :

MURPHY (roman) 1947

SAMUEL BECKETT

MOLLOY

☆
m

LES EDITIONS DE MINUIT
PARIS

88

SAMUEL BECKETT

MOLLOY

a novel
translated from the French
by Patrick Bowles
in collaboration with the Author

[handwritten inscription]

COLLECTION MERLIN

THE OLYMPIA PRESS
8 rue de Nesle, Paris, 6°

94

98

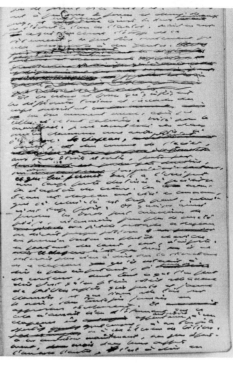

94. *Molloy.* A novel translated from the French by Patrick Bowles in collaboration with the author. Paris: Collection Merlin, The Olympia Press [1955]. 12mo, original plain wrappers with printed paper cover.

Inscribed on the title page: "First European edition / of Patrick Bowles's / translation of Molloy / for / Jake Schwartz / Sam. Beckett."

95. *Molloy.* A novel translated from the French by Patrick Bowles in collaboration with the author. New York: Grove Press (1955). 8vo, original cloth, dust jacket. First American edition. Signed by Beckett on the title page.

96. *Molloy.* A novel translated from the French by Patrick Bowles in collaboration with the author. New York: Grove Press (1955). 8vo, original illustrated wrappers.

Inscribed on the title page: "first American edition / of Patrick Bowles's trans- / lation of *Molloy.* / for Jake Schwartz / Sam. Beckett."

97. *Molloy.* Translated from the French by Samuel Beckett and Patrick Bowles. London: Calder and Boyars (1966). First English edition.

98. "Malone Meurt." Autograph manuscript, signed, dated at the beginning, 27 November 1947; dated upon completion, 30 May 1948, 322 pp., folio.

Written in various colored inks in two notebooks, the first of which contains the final sections of *Watt.* With autograph revisions, additions, and deletions, and a number of characteristic doodles and mathematical calculations. Both notebooks bear the original title, "L'Absent." The inside back covers, flyleaves, and final pages have notes in English and in French pertaining to *Watt* and to "L'Absent."
On the cover of the second notebook Beckett has written: "L'Absent—Original title of *Malone Meurt.* Part I in Watt VI [*sic*] Notebook. Samuel Beckett. This concludes original MS."
This manuscript, like the one for *Molloy,* is dated at regular intervals throughout—with less frequency, however.

99. "Malone s'en conte." In *84: Nouvelle Revue Littéraire,* No. 16 (December 1950). Paris: Les Editions de Minuit. 8vo, original wrappers, uncut.

Beckett has signed the extract below the title. The text has a few manuscript corrections.

100. "Quel Malheur." In *Les Temps Modernes,* 7ᵉ année, No. 71 (September 1951). Crown 8vo, original printed wrappers, uncut and partially unopened.

This extract from *Malone Meurt,* printed in Sartre's review one month before the novel was published by Les Editions de Minuit, contains variants from the Minuit edition. Beckett has written, at the beginning of the extract, "for John & Evelyn [Kobler] / with love from Sam / Paris April 1972."

101. *Malone Meurt.* [Paris] Les Editions de Minuit (1951). 12mo, original wrappers, uncut and unopened.

> First edition. One of 47 numbered copies on *vélin du Ghaldwell.* Inscribed on the half-title: "for John [Kobler] from Sam / Paris April 1966."

102. _____. Another copy of the first edition, this one on ordinary paper, unnumbered.

> Inscribed on the half-title: "for / Jake Schwartz / from / Samuel Beckett / Paris May 1956."

Malone Meurt. See also No. 364.

103. "Malone Dies." Carbon copy of typed manuscript, signed, with autograph emendations throughout, 159 pp., 4to.

> Title written out, in Beckett's hand: "Malone Dies / By / Samuel Beckett / Translated from the original French by the author."
> An autograph note beneath Beckett's signature reads: "corrections in / my hand"; another one, below the title: "published by Grove Press, / N.Y. 1956."

104. "Malone Dies. From the Author's Translation of *Malone Meurt.*" In *Irish Writing,* No. 34 (Spring 1956). Editor: S. J. White. 8vo, original printed wrappers. Beckett has signed the extract above the title.

105. *Malone Dies.* A novel translated from the French by the author. New York: Grove Press (1956). 8vo, original pictorial wrappers.

> Inscribed on the title page: "first edition of my / translation of *Malone Meurt* / for Jake Schwartz / Sam. Beckett."

106. *Malone Dies.* A novel translated from the French by the author. New York: Grove Press (1956). 8vo, original cloth. One of the hard-bound limited edition of 500 numbered copies. Signed by Beckett on the title page.

107. *Malone Dies.* A novel translated from the French by the author. London: John Calder (1958). 8vo, original cloth, dust jacket.

> Inscribed by Beckett on the title page: "for Hugo Manning / with all good wishes / from Samuel Beckett / Paris March 1972."
> With the L. W. Payne bookplate.

108. *Malone Dies.* A novel translated from the French by the author. [Harmondsworth] Penguin Books (1962). 12mo, original pictorial wrappers.

109. "L'Innommable." Autograph manuscript, signed, begun 29 March 1949, completed at Ussy, January 1950, 284 pp., folio.

> Written in ink and in pencil in two cloth-bound ledgers. With

MALONE MEURT

102 103

MALONE DIES
By
Samuel Beckett
Translated from the original French by the author.

I shall soon be quite dead at last in spite of all. Perhaps next month. Then it will be the month of April or of May. For the year is still young, a thousand little signs tell me so. Perhaps I am wrong, perhaps I shall survive Saint John the Baptist's Day and even the Fourteenth of July, festival of freedom. Indeed I would not put it past me to pant on to the Transfiguration, not to speak of the Assumption. But I do not think so, I do not think I am wrong in saying that these rejoicings will take place in my absence, this year. I have that feeling, I have had it now for some days, and I credit it. But in what does it differ from those that have abused me ever since I was born? No, that is the kind of bait I do not rise to any more, my need for prettiness is gone. I could die to-day, if I wished, merely by making a little effort, if I could wish, if I could make an effort. But it is just as well to let myself die, quietly, without rushing things. Something must have changed. I will not weigh upon the balance any more, one way or the other. I shall be neutral and inert. No difficulty there. Throes are the only trouble, I must be on my guard against throes. But I am less given to them now, since coming here. Of course I still have my little fits of impatience, from time to time, I must be on my guard against them, for the next fortnight or three weeks. Without exaggeration to be sure, quietly crying and laughing, without working myself up into a state. Yes, I shall be natural at last,

109

autograph deletions and emendations throughout. The flyleaf of Notebook I has an autograph note: "This is the original MS / of *L'Innommable* / written 1949–50 and / published by the Editions / de Minuit May 1953. / Samuel Beckett / in 2 notebooks." Two 4to sheets of autograph text and corrections are tipped in at the end. Autograph notes inside back cover.

110. "Mahood" [an excerpt from *L'Innommable*]. In *La Nouvelle Nouvelle Revue Française*, 1ère année, No. 2 (1 February 1953). 8vo, original printed wrappers, uncut and unopened.

La Nouvelle Revue Française, the most prestigious of the French literary monthlies, had started publishing in 1909 (after a false start in November 1908). André Gide was its principal founding father, abetted by Jacques Copeau, Jacques Rivière, Jean Schlumberger, Marcel Drouin, Henri Ghéon, and André Ruyters. The review suspended publication, under the German occupation, in 1943. Starting again, finally, ten years later, under the new style *La Nouvelle Nouvelle Revue Française*, it continued to include among its contributors the established names of the period (Saint-John Perse, André Malraux, Léon-Paul Fargue, for example) but welcomed the new writers who had only recently begun to make their mark: Maurice Blanchot, Roger Caillois, Henry Miller, Arthur Adamov, and, of course, Samuel Beckett.

110 1er FÉVRIER 1953   1ère ANNÉE No 2

LA NOUVELLE

NOUVELLE
REVUE FRANÇAISE

VALERY LARBAUD	Pages de Journal
JEAN GRENIER	L'époque des Sibylles
SAMUEL BECKETT	Mahood
ROGER CAILLOIS	Guerre et Démocratie
JACQUES CHARDONNE	Antoine
SAINT-JOHN PERSE	Amers (fin)
ANDRÉ DHÔTEL	Les premiers Temps (1)

— CHRONIQUES —

Continuez autant qu'il vous plaira, par MAURICE BLANCHOT
Jean Vilar et le Théâtre de la Cruauté, par JEAN DUVIGNAUD
Les Dangers de la Vertu, par DOMINIQUE AURY
Sainte-Beuve, par MARCEL ARLAND

— NOTES —

par M. ARLAND, D. AURY, Y. BELAVAL, M. COURNOT, ETIEMBLE, F. GÉRARD, G. LAMBRICHS, J. PAULHAN, M. RAINOIRD, ROLLAND DE RENÉVILLE.

La Poésie. — *Hélène, ou le règne végétal*, par René-Guy Cadou. — *Louisfert-en-Poésie*, par Michel Manoll.
Les Essais. — *Le mythe de Rimbaud*, par Etiemble. — *Saint Genet, comédien et martyr*, par Jean-Paul Sartre.
Lettres Étrangères. — *Les Papiers, de Boswell. — Le vieil homme et la mer*, par E. Hemingway.
Les Arts. — *Art religieux et Art sacré. — L'Exposition Geer van Velde. — Peinture et Société* par P. Francastel.
Revues et Journaux : Éluard aux Cahiers du Sud. — La Parisienne. — Au pilon !
Revue des Livres.

— LE TEMPS, COMME IL PASSE —

CH. A. CINGRIA : Chronique
MARCEL JOUHANDEAU : Galande
AUDIBERTI : Une bombe rue Visconti
ANDRÉ PIEYRE DE MANDIARGUES : Le dogme de Cham

— TEXTES —

MARCEL PROUST : La femme de chambre de la Baronne de Picpus
Introduction, par BERNARD DE FALLOIS

FRANCE : 195 FR.   nrf

to believe this or that, the point is to guess right, nothing more, they say, if it's not white it's probably black, it must be admitted this method lacks subtlety, in view of the _____ _____ equally worthy of _____ a chance. The time they waste repeating the same thing, when they must know _____ it's not the right one. Recriminations easily _____, if they chose to take the trouble, _____ the _____ to reflect on their insanity. _____ think about what you have said, _____ at the same time _____ you think about any old thing, you say any old thing, more or less, more or less, _____ that's why they you can't _____ _____ always repeat the same thing, the same old litany, the one they know by heart, _____ to try and _____ think of something different, _____ of a _____ to say something different from the same old thing, always the same wrong thing said always wrong, they can _____ of nothing, _____ nothing else to say but the thing that prevents them _____, they'd _____ better _____ to think _____ what they're saying, in order _____ vary it's presentation _____, _____ _____ _____, but how can _____ think and say _____ at the same time, _____ _____ special _____, _____ thoughts wander, _____ words too, far apart, no, that's an exageration, apart, between them would be the place to be, where you suffer, rejoice, at being bereft of speech, bereft of thought, and feel nothing, hear nothing, know nothing, say nothing, are nothing, that would be a blessed place to be, where you are. it's a lucky thing they are there, _____ _____ anywhere _____, to bear the responsibility of this state of affairs, with respect to which if one does not know a great deal one knows at least this, that one would not care to have it on one's conscience, to have it on one's stomach is enough. Yes, I'm a lucky man to have them, these volubly shades, _____ the little rascals, I won't have them _____, I feel it, they'll make me _____

Decreasing indestructible HEAP for Jaque ...

MOLLOY,
MALONE DIES,
and THE UNNAMABLE

THREE NOVELS BY

Samuel Beckett

GROVE PRESS, INC.   NEW YORK

111. *L'Innommable.* [Paris] Les Editions de Minuit (1953). 12mo, original wrappers, uncut and unopened.

> One of 50 numbered copies on *vélin supérieur.*
> Inscribed on the title page: "for John [Kobler] / from Sam / Paris April / 1966."

112. "The Unnamable." Autograph manuscript, signed, started February 1957, completed 23 February 1958, 253 pp., small 4to, in morocco-backed folding box.

> Written in blue and red inks in three notebooks. Each notebook has, in Beckett's hand, the title, number of the notebook, and the note, "original manuscript of the author's translation." The second notebook has the additional phrase (title?) *"Beyond words?"* The last manuscript page of the third notebook bears the inscription: "This is the original MS of my translation of *L'Innommable* / For my friend Jake Schwartz, / with my best wishes. / Samuel Beckett / March 1958."
> With autograph revisions and doodles (some very intricate) throughout. One of these doodles, at the exact midpoint of the second notebook, depicts a kind of piscine being from whose mouth emerges a balloon containing the autograph notation (in French), "Began work again 21.1.58 after failure of *Henry et Ada.*" This is a reference to Beckett's radio play *Embers,* to work on which he had apparently interrupted this translation. (Prior to this point the manuscript is in blue ink; from here on, in red.) It is curious (but not at all uncharacteristic) that Beckett should have seen as a failure (*"échec"*) a play which the following year, after its performance on the BBC, was awarded the Italia Prize for 1959. (See No. 266.)

113. "The Unnamable." Typed manuscript (some carbon copy), completed June 1958, 150 pp., 4to, half-morocco, raised bands, top edges gilt.

> Heavily revised, mostly in Beckett's hand. On page 1, Beckett has written, "1st revision up to p. 25."
> The typescript includes carbon copies of the extracts sent to the *Chicago Review* and *The Texas Quarterly,* so designated in Beckett's hand (and one other).

114. "[Extract from] *The Unnamable.*" Typed manuscript, 4 pp., 4to.

> With several revisions, in black ink, in Beckett's hand, and with a few blue-crayon indications to the printer in another.
> Typescript submitted to *The Texas Quarterly,* Vol. I, No. 2 (Spring 1958). This is the ribbon copy of the carbon typescript entitled "Extract from *The Unnamable*" and marked in Beckett's hand "Texas Review" which he incorporated, with further revision, into a later typescript of the full work. Beckett has deleted "Extract from" in the title of the typescript sent to *The Texas Quarterly* and has added at the end of the excerpt "(Translated by the author from the original French.)."

115. Documents relating to the extract of *The Unnamable* printed in *The Texas Quarterly:*

(a) Typed manuscript, signed, of David Hayman's introduction to Beckett's text, with revisions in black ink, blue crayon, and pencil, 3 pp., 4to;

(b) typed manuscript of Beckett's text, together with Hayman's introduction, marked in blue crayon and in pencil with instructions to the printer, 11 pp., 4to;

(c) proof sheets, from *The Texas Quarterly*, of Beckett's text and Hayman's introduction. With two corrections, 5 pp., 4to.

116. "The Unnamable." Translated from French by the author. With an introduction by David Hayman. In *The Texas Quarterly*, Vol. I, No. 2 (Spring 1958). Harry Ransom, Editor. Austin: University of Texas Press. 4to, original pictorial wrappers. Beckett has signed his name at the end of the extract.

117. "Excerpt: The Unnamable." Translated by the author from the original French. In *Chicago Review*, Vol. XII, No. 2 (Summer 1958). 8vo, original pictorial wrappers.

A prepublication excerpt, varying slightly from the Grove Press first edition.

118. "The Unnamable" [extract]. In *Spectrum*, Vol. II, No. 1 (Winter 1958). 8vo, original printed wrappers.

Inscribed on the front cover: "for Jake Schwartz / from Sam. Beckett / Paris 1958."

119. *The Unnamable*. Translated from the French by the author. New York: Grove Press (1958). 8vo, original linen-backed cloth. First American edition. One of a specially bound and signed issue of 26 lettered copies.

120. *Molloy, Malone Dies, and The Unnamable*. Three Novels by Samuel Beckett. New York: Grove Press (1959). 8vo, original cloth, dust jacket (with photograph of Samuel Beckett by Brassaï).

First collected edition.
Inscribed boldly in pencil on the title page: "Decreasing / indestruct-ible / HEAP / for Jaque / Les Iles Marquises / Feb. 1960 / Sam."
The provenance of this book would indicate that "Jaque" was "Jake" [Schwartz] – "tipsily spelt" (S.B.). That identification is reinforced by the locus of the inscription: a restaurant in the Rue de la Gaîté, across from Bobino, much frequented, at an earlier period, by theater people, sundry sporting types, and amateurs of Dover sole. Jake Schwartz had lifted a glass there with Beckett on earlier convivial occasions in Paris.
The "decreasing indestructible heap," Mr. Beckett has pointed out elsewhere, is a reference to the "old Sophist teaser (sorites): When is a heap not a heap? By subtraction of how many grains? Conversely, when become a heap? By adjunction of how many?" Which leads to Hamm's soliloquy in *Endgame*: "Moment upon moment, pattering

down, like the millet grains of . . . that old Greek." (Grove Press Evergreen edition, p. 70).

121. *Molloy. Malone Dies. The Unnamable.* London: John Calder (1959) [1960]. In collaboration with Olympia Press, Paris. 8vo, original boards, dust jacket.

First English collected edition.
Inscribed on the title page: "for Jake Schwartz / his friend / Sam. Beckett / Paris Sept. 1960."

122. William York Tindall. "Beckett's Bums." Typed manuscript, signed, 25 January–2 February 1958, 16 pp., 4to.

Heavily revised text of the "Ms in progress" of the plaquette published by T. E. Hanley in 1960. With a presentation inscription to Jake [Schwartz]. Attached is a photocopy of a letter from Professor Tindall, of Columbia University, to T. E. Hanley: "I am convinced that Beckett is the best living writer. . . . My judgment has been formed by Joyce, Yeats, Thomas. In my opinion Beckett is right up there with these giants."
Professor Tindall was one of a group of academics who resolutely and persistently recommended Beckett for the Nobel Prize during the 1960s.

123. William York Tindall. *Beckett's Bums.* Privately printed, 1960. 8vo, original wrappers, uncut. One of 70 copies "printed and distributed for the friends of T.E.H. [T. E. Hanley]."

EN ATTENDANT GODOT
WAITING FOR GODOT

There are watersheds in the theater that, overnight, send history scurrying off in new directions. *Hernani*, at the Comédie Française on 25 February 1830, was one. *Ubu Roi*, at the Théâtre de l'Oeuvre on 10 December 1896, was another (bringing forth from Yeats, "After us the savage God"); *Le Sacre du printemps*, *Parade*, and *Les Mamelles de Tirésias*, likewise, in their time.

En attendant Godot, which opened at the Théâtre de Babylone on 5 January 1953 and from there soon made its way around the world, established Samuel Beckett as the most original and significant dramatist of our time.

Godot has been oversimply described as a play "about two tramps waiting nowhere in particular for someone who never shows up." The play, whatever it is "about," has recast the face of theater in our time. But theater managers didn't exactly fight for the privilege of producing it. Tristan Tzara had talked about *Godot* to Roger Blin, an actor-director well-known in the Paris avant-garde theater. Blin read the play. He caught a glimpse of something that appealed to him. He didn't, as he admitted later on, see it all, by any means. Long afterward he met Beckett and—like Jean Thomas and others—found him somewhat "intimidating." They talked about *Godot*, in particular about the technical problems it raised, very little about its "meaning." It was only when they began to rehearse, at the Théâtre de Babylone, that what Blin has called its "richness" began to emerge for him and his fellow actors. Beckett followed the rehearsals very closely. Blin remembers that period as a happy, boisterous time. No one got very involved with the metaphysical aspects of the play. But under its mask of bleakness Blin became aware that they were nourishing a tiny, insistent spark: the will to live, the love of life, and it became for all of them a joyous, triumphal experience.

Jérôme Lindon had already published *Godot* by the time it was finally produced. But once produced and immediately and simultaneously a *succès de scandale* and a *pièce à succès*, it ran on in France, then moved through Germany and Italy, England, Ireland, the United States—the world—to cheer, trouble, and awe hearts and minds as few other plays of modern times (from among those not designed for popular consumption) have done.

Godot is a play of inexhaustible provocation and resonance. It defies explanation, although the ever-growing mass of exegetical commentary offers many. Some spectators, accustomed to more traditional fare, found it boring; others, confusing and, because they could not feel sure of its meaning, frustrating. But many more found it quite beautiful, this spectacle of two tramps—Beckett had not visualized them as such—waiting endlessly for Godot, who never arrives (who, what is Godot? Beckett offers no clues); they sensed the indomitable will to believe, the need to press on, not to give up in the face of delay and disappointment. The excitement is in Beckett's mastery of language, its calculated discontinuities, its incongruous conjunctures, all brought into balance by the sure hand of a sublime magician thoroughly at home in the theater. The language is not literary but real. It marked a new direction for French theater, a clean break with the past.

There were repeated delays in getting *Godot* onto the boards: director, actors, theater, subsidies—all the usual problems, plus a few more stemming from the uncompromising face it showed to the world.

"The play held up for want of funds," Beckett wrote Susan Manning on 4 October 1951. "More interested in carrots than in literature at the moment." But by mid-April 1953, he was able to give her a rosier rundown that included performances in Lyons and Brussels, the 100th in Paris, a German tour, and "talk of New York." He had "made a good deal of money with it already (more, in a couple of months, than with all my other writings put together)."

Later, on 22 June, he wrote to Mary Manning Howe that he had been "translating the brute into approximate English for possible performance in N.Y." With *Godot* being put on in Geneva, he added, and "all over Germany too at the same time, perhaps I'll be able to buy a carpet and a refrigerator." By 18 August 1955 (in another letter to Mrs. Howe), he was "really tired of *Godot*, and the endless misunderstanding it provokes everywhere." It was obvious that he had a bear by the tail.

The Miami "fiasco"—the American premiere—he wrote to Reavey on 11 January 1956, "is unimportant and leaves me cold as camphor." Two months later he wrote to Susan Manning, "For the past five years I suffer from a chronic loathing of all that trickles from my pen. Perhaps it is time I called it a day. . . . I don't know what they are doing or planning to do with Godot in New York and don't much care. . . . Sometimes I wonder if I ever knew what it was to want to do something." Life would never be the same again.

124. ["En attendant Godot"]. Autograph manuscript, fair copy, with minor corrections, 156 pp. The text has been written on small-4to pages removed from an exercise book and tipped onto blank sheets of white drawing paper.

   The original autograph manuscript of *En attendant Godot* still belongs to its author. The present copy was made by him for Jake Schwartz, a dentist-turned-bookseller, who sold it to T. E. Hanley, of Bradford, Pennsylvania, one of the major American collectors of twentieth-century rare books and manuscripts. Hanley's library was purchased by The University of Texas in several installments, beginning in 1958.

125. *En attendant Godot. Pièce en deux actes.* [Paris] Les Editions de Minuit, 1952. 8vo, original wrappers, uncut. First edition. One of 35 numbered large-paper copies on *vélin supérieur.*

124   126

DU MÊME AUTEUR

☆m

MOLLOY, roman.

MALONE MEURT, roman.

L'INNOMMABLE, roman (à paraître).

SAMUEL BECKETT

En attendant
Godot

PIÈCE EN DEUX ACTES

☆m

LES ÉDITIONS DE MINUIT
1952

125

126. *En attendant Godot. Pièce en deux actes.* [Paris] Les Editions de Minuit, 1952 [1954]. 8vo, original wrappers, uncut.

Second edition, photographically reprinted. Unlike the first edition, this one is illustrated with six photographs taken from productions of *Godot* in Germany. (At the end of the play's second run in Paris, in September 1953, Roger Blin had taken the original cast on tour through France, Switzerland, Italy, and Germany.)
This copy, from Nancy Cunard's library, is inscribed on the half-title: "for / Nancy / with love from / Samuel / Paris April 1956."

127. *En attendant Godot. Pièce en deux actes.* [Paris] Les Editions de Minuit, 1952 [1956]. 8vo, original wrappers, uncut and unopened.

This large-paper copy, one of 30 numbered copies on *Alfama*, is the third edition of *Godot* and is illustrated with six photographs from the German productions of the play. In the decade following the first printing of *Godot*, there were a number of photographic reprints, with and without plates.

128. *En attendant Godot. Pièce en deux actes.* Edited by Colin Duckworth. With a foreword by Harold Hobson. London, Toronto, Wellington, and Sidney: George G. Harrap & Co. (1966). 12mo, original boards.

An educational edition, with critical essays, bibliography, and notes by Colin Duckworth. Illustrated with photographs from various productions of the play.

129. *En attendant Godot.* Frankfurt am Main: Verlag Moritz Diesterweg (1971). 12mo, original wrappers, illustrated with a scene from one of the German productions of *Godot*.

Educational edition, with an introduction and notes by Joachim Thiel.
Inscribed on the title page: "for John & Evelyn [Kobler] / with love from Sam / Paris April 1972."

En attendant Godot. See also No. 263.

130. "Waiting for Godot." Autograph manuscript, signed, 165 pp., written in two small-4to notebooks.

This manuscript of Beckett's translation of *Godot* into English, not the original, shows a substantial number of variants, omissions, and corrections from the printed text.

131. *Waiting for Godot. Tragicomedy in Two Acts.* Translated from the original French text by the author. New York: Grove Press (1954). 8vo, original black cloth. Illustrated with photographs from a production given in Germany by the original Paris cast.

First edition in English.
Inscribed on the title page: "for Jake Schwartz / cordially / Samuel Beckett / Paris June 1956."

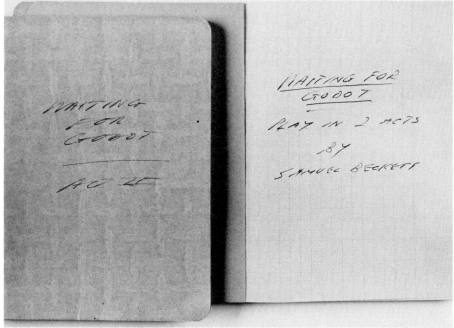

130

132. *Waiting for Godot. Tragicomedy in Two Acts.* Translated from the original French text by the author. New York: Grove Press (1954). 8vo, original pictorial wrappers.

  Soft-cover issue of the first edition in English, with variant wrappers, on uncoated stock and with a portion of Harold Hobson's review of the London production of *Godot* on the back cover.
  From the library of the theater historian and critic John Gassner, with his signature on the front flyleaf.

133. *Waiting for Godot. Tragicomedy in Two Acts.* Translated from the original French text by the author. New York: Grove Press (1954). 8vo, original pictorial wrappers on coated stock.

  Soft-cover issue of the first edition in English.
  From the library of the playwright Elmer Rice.

134. _____. Another copy, from the library of the stage manager Robert Downing.

135. "Waiting for Godot." In *Theatre Arts*, Vol. XL, No. 8 (August 1956). Folio, original pictorial wrappers.

  The complete text of *Godot*, illustrated with photographs from the New York and London productions. An article by Alan Levy, "The Long Wait for Godot," precedes it.

136. *Waiting for Godot. Tragicomedy in Two Acts.* New York: Grove Press (1970). 8vo, original black cloth with gilt lettering. First printing in the

series *The Collected Works of Samuel Beckett.* One of 200 numbered copies, signed by Samuel Beckett.

137. *Waiting for Godot.* With fourteen original etchings by Dellas Henke. (Iowa City, 1979). Folio, loose in sheets, within sleeve and folding box.

The edition, limited to 40 copies on Arches paper, was printed by the artist between May 1977 and July 1979. The types, Bembo and Centaur, were handset by Margaret Zillioux-Henke. Each of the full-page etchings is numbered and signed. Laid in are three original drawings, preparatory studies for illustrations: two in ink and one in pencil.
This is one of seven copies signed by Samuel Beckett.

138. *Waiting for Godot. A Tragicomedy in Two Acts.* London: Faber and Faber (1956). 8vo, original ocher cloth.

First English edition. Presentation copy inscribed: "for / Jake Schwartz / sincerely / Samuel Beckett June 1956."
The first British production of *Waiting for Godot* was a private one, at the Arts Theatre Club in London, under the direction of Peter Hall. In order for the play to be performed publicly, however, Beckett's text had to withstand a close reading by the Lord Chamberlain, the official censor—"His Nibs," as Beckett later referred to him. Needless to say, Beckett's characters and the Lord Chamberlain spoke different languages and before *Godot* could open at the Criterion Theatre, British prudery exacted its toll. Entire passages were cut, such as the one which connects hanging and erections, and another which refers to an unbuttoned fly. In other instances, "objectionable" words were replaced by less "offensive" terminology—the mother of the Gozzo family, for example, had "warts" rather than "the clap."
It wasn't until December 1964—after the office of the Lord Chamberlain had finally gone out of business—that the unexpurgated version of *Godot* was performed, with official British sanction, at the Royal Court Theatre in London, under Beckett's supervision. A tipped-in publisher's note explains the censored text as follows: "When *Waiting for Godot* was transferred from the Arts Theatre to the Criterion Theatre, a small number of textual deletions were made to satisfy the requirements of the Lord Chamberlain. The text printed here is that used in the Criterion Theatre production."

139. _____. Another copy of the London first edition, with original illustrated dust jacket.

140. *Waiting for Godot. A Tragicomedy in Two Acts.* London: Samuel French (1957). Crown 8vo, original blue-and-white wrappers.

In this acting edition, the text of the play contains, in addition to Beckett's stage directions, more detailed instructions concerning the actors' movements.

141. *Waiting for Godot. A Tragicomedy in Two Acts.* London: Faber and Faber (1959). 12mo, original printed wrappers, varying from those called for by Federman and Fletcher. First English paperback edition. Signed by Beckett on the title page.

142. *Waiting for Godot. A Tragicomedy in Two Acts.* London: Faber and Faber (1965). 8vo, original pale ocher cloth, dust jacket.

Second English edition, revised and unexpurgated. Signed by Beckett on the title page.

An announcement on the inside flap of the dust jacket reads: "The author has made a number of important revisions to the text of *Waiting for Godot* since it was first published and this new edition, complete and unexpurgated, has been authorized by Mr. Beckett as definitive."

143. *Waiting for Godot. A Tragicomedy in Two Acts.* London: Faber and Faber (1971). 12mo, original illustrated wrappers.

An educational edition, with afterword and notes by John Fletcher.
Inscribed on the title page: "for John & Evelyn [Kobler] / with love from Sam / Paris april / 1972."

144. *Warten auf Godot.* [Berlin] Suhrkamp Verlag, 1953. 12mo, original printed wrappers.

First German edition.
Inscribed on the title page: "Widely performed / in Germany / for Jake Schwartz / Sam. Beckett."

Nos. 127-129, 131, 134, 136, 138, 140-145, 147-150

71

137

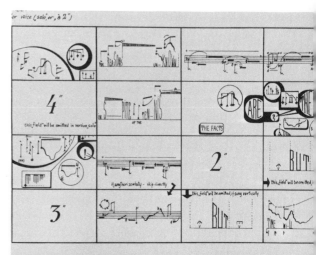

152

154

153

145. *Warten auf Godot. En attendant Godot. Waiting for Godot.* [Frankfurt am Main] Suhrkamp (1971). 12mo, original wrappers.

Trilingual edition, inscribed on the title page: "for John and Evelyn [Kobler] / with love from Sam / Paris April / 1972."

146. *Beckett. Warten auf Godot. Schiller-Theater* [Berlin, 1975]. 8vo, original printed wrappers.

Illustrated brochure describing and picturing the rehearsals for the Berlin production of *Warten auf Godot* at the Schiller-Theater in 1975.
On 8 January 1975, Beckett wrote to Reavey, "Here since late December directing *Godot* for the Schiller Theater (and my sins). If this doesn't purge them nothing will.... We open—if ever—early March."

147. *Aspettando Godot.* Translated by Carlo Fruttero. [Torino] Giulio Einaudi editore, 1956. 12mo, original pictorial wrappers, uncut and unopened.

First Italian edition.
Inscribed on the title page: "This is the original / Italian translation / for / Jake Schwartz / Sam. Beckett / performed in Rome."

148. [Japanese translation of] *En attendant Godot.* [Tokyo] Hakusuisha [1956]. Illustrated. 12mo, original decorative wrappers.

First Japanese edition.
Inscribed by Beckett: "This is the original / Japanese translation / for / Jake Schwartz / Sam. Beckett."

149. *I väntan på Godot. Pjäs i två akter.* Stockholm: Albert Bonniers Förlag (1957). 12mo, original wrappers, uncut and unopened.

First Swedish edition.
Inscribed on the title page: "First Swedish edition / of *Waiting for Godot* / for Jake Schwartz / Sam. Beckett / Paris Sept. 1957."

150. *Mens vi venter på Godot.* In *Samuel Beckett. Skuespiel.* Oslo: Gyldendal Norsk Forlag (1968). 12mo, original pictorial wrappers. First Norwegian edition of *En attendant Godot.*

151. *Voices. From the play "Waiting for Godot" by Samuel Beckett.* Score. Set to music by Marc Wilkinson, for contralto voice, flute, E_b clarinet, bass clarinet, and violoncello. Words in English and German. [London] Universal Edition [1960]. Crown 8vo, original wrappers.

152. *Credentials or "Think, Think Lucky."* Score, by Roman Haubenstock-Ramati for Lucky's monologue from *Waiting for Godot*, for voice, piano, celesta, vibraphone and bells, violin, clarinet, trombone, and percussion. Introduction in English and German. [Vienna] Universal Edition. Commissioned by SWF Baden-Baden, Germany, 1961. Oblong folio, original wrappers.

153. Two photographs from the first Broadway production of *Waiting for Godot* at the John Golden Theatre in 1956, with Alvin Epstein as Lucky, Bert Lahr as Estragon, Kurt Kasznar as Pozzo, and E. G. Marshall as Vladimir, directed by Herbert Berghof; together with a playbill.

154. Three photographs of the 1971 Alan Schneider production of *Waiting for Godot* at the Sheridan Square Playhouse in Greenwich Village, showing the actors who played Estragon and Vladimir during the run: Paul B. Price, Henderson Forsythe, Oliver Clark, Joey Faye, and Tom Ewell; together with a playbill.

155. Two photographs of the cast of the 1975 production of *Warten auf Godot* at the Schiller-Theater Werkstatt, Berlin, supervised by Beckett himself. Inscribed by all the members of the group and dated 8 Marz 1975.

156. Suzanne Dumesnil. "F_____." Translated from the original French by Samuel Beckett. In *Transition Forty-Eight*, No. 4 (15 January 1949). 12mo, original pictorial wrappers.

A short story by Beckett's wife, written at the time Beckett was writing *En attendant Godot*. The translation is unsigned.

155

Beckett wrote *Watt*, "the last stuttering in English," during World War II, the second half while he was living in the village of Roussillon, in the Vaucluse. But it was not published until 1953, after the appearance of his trilogy and of *En attendant Godot*, all of which had been written in French.

In a letter to George Reavey, Beckett wrote from Foxrock: "It is an unsatisfactory book, written in dribs and drabs, first on the run, then of an evening after the clodhopping, during the occupation. But it has its place in the series, as will perhaps appear in time." And elsewhere to Reavey: "My book *Watt* has been turned down by Routledge. Mr. Ragg and Mr. Read agreed that it was 'wild and unintelligible' and felt very sorry for the author of *Murphy*. . . . If you knew of any agent, preferably young, with even half the tenacity you displayed in handling *Murphy* I should be glad to know his name." Beckett eventually decided to stay with Reavey, however, and *Watt* began making the rounds of the other English publishers. Beckett's friend Denis Devlin returned to his Washington diplomatic post, taking a typescript with him to try the American market. There was little real progress on either front. Finally Richard Seaver, an editor of the Paris review *Merlin*, after reading *Molloy* and *Malone Meurt*, wrote to Beckett in the hope of extracting from him a text of some kind for his magazine. After several unsuccessful attempts to get in touch with Beckett, Seaver answered a knock at his door one day and found him there, with the manuscript of *Watt*. Beckett handed it to him and left—"almost without a word." The *Merlin* team was exuberantly enthusiastic but barely solvent. With the collaboration of Maurice Girodias who, like his father before him (Jack Kahane), published, chiefly, books unpublishable in the United States and England (e.g., Henry Miller), they brought out, in 1953, with a dual imprint, the eminently respectable—almost chaste—*Watt*.

157. "Watt." Autograph manuscript, signed, 1940–1945, 945 pp. Written in ink and colored crayons, in six notebooks, folio, 4to, and small 4to, and on loose sheets, some laid in notebooks, some separate.

With many changes, deletions, and additions, and numerous doodles, sketches, mathematical calculations, rhyming schemes, and drawings. The first notebook is signed and marked "Watt I," with the following note: "*Watt* was written in France during the war 1940–45 and published in 1953 by the Olympia Press." On an inserted sheet, Beckett has written, "Begun evening of Tuesday 11/2/41." The first page of the second notebook is dated "3/12/41." Notebook 3 shows the date "5.5.42" on the first page of text. The cover of the fourth notebook is marked "Poor Johnny / Watt / Roussillon," and page 1 is headed,

"Roussillon, October 4th 1943." On the cover of Notebook 5 Beckett has written, in variously colored inks, "Watt V / Suite et fin / 18.2.45 / Paris / Et début de *L'Absent* / Novembre-Janvier 47/48." He has indicated that *L'Absent* is *Malone Meurt*. Page 99 has the note, "End of continuation of Watt. Conclusion in Notebook VI." Although in Notebook I, Beckett placed the completion of *Watt* in 1945, he concludes the sixth notebook with "Dec 28th 1944 / End."

Watt is a whale of a manuscript—a white whale. Among the thousands of modern manuscripts in the Humanities Research Center, it glows like a luminous secular relic. It is, at moments, magnificently ornate, a worthy scion of The Book of Kells, with the colors reduced to more somber hues. The doodles, cartoons, caricatures, portraits *en cartouche* include reminiscences of African and Oceanic art, the gargoyles of Notre-Dame, heraldry, and more. Beckett's handwriting is at its most deceptively cursive. *Eppur si legge!* And it "reads" in other ways, too. Jorge Luis Borges, examining *Watt* tactilely, along with manuscripts by Poe and Whitman, Baudelaire and other favorites of his, sensed something of its extraordinary qualities, which, obviously, must transcend the visual. He asked his companion to describe it to him. This she did in detail, Borges nodding, "Yes, yes," with a happy smile throughout her description.

158. "Watt." Typed manuscript (some carbon copy), signed, 297 pp., 4to and folio.

   Marked at the beginning, "Original typescript of / *Watt* Incomplete / Samuel Beckett." With numerous autograph revisions and deletions, in ink, colored crayons, and pencil. Some doodles and mathematical calculations. With substantial differences from the published text.

159. "An Extract from *Watt*." In *Envoy: A Review of Literature and Art*, Vol. I, No. 2 (January 1950). 8vo, original illustrated wrappers, uncut.

160. "Extract from *Watt*." In *Irish Writing*, No. 17 (December 1951). Edited by David Marcus and Terence Smith. 8vo, original illustrated wrappers, uncut. Signed by Beckett at the beginning of the extract.

161. "Extract from *Watt*." In *Merlin*, Vol. I, No. 3 (Winter 1952–53). Edited by Alexander Trocchi. Advisory Editor and Director: Richard Seaver. Crown 8vo, original wrappers.

   Inscribed by Beckett: "This extract appeared shortly / before publication of *Watt* / by the Olympia Press, Paris / for Jake Schwartz / Samuel Beckett."

162. "Extract from *Watt*." In *Irish Writing*, No. 22 (March 1953). 8vo, original wrappers, uncut. Signed by Beckett at the beginning of the extract.

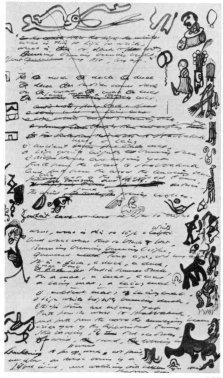

157   158

163. *Watt.* Paris: Collection Merlin, The Olympia Press, 1953. 8vo, original wrappers, uncut and unopened.

> First edition.
> Large-paper copy, marked "S," one of 25 copies printed "on fine paper," lettered, and signed by Beckett. The total edition consisted of 1,125 copies. The title page bears the inscription: "for Jake Schwartz / Sam Beckett."
> Laid in is the original Olympia Press announcement for publication of *Watt* in the "Collection Merlin."

164. *Watt.* Paris: Collection Merlin, The Olympia Press, 1953. 12mo, original magenta wrappers, uncut.

> This copy is one of the regular edition of 1,100 numbered copies. It bears Beckett's signature on the title page.

165. *Watt.* Paris: The Olympia Press (1958). 12mo, original boards, dust jacket.

> Second edition, in The Traveller's Companion series.
> Inscribed by Beckett on the half-title: "for Jake [Schwartz] / from his friend / Sam / Paris May 1958."

166. *Watt.* New York: Grove Press (1959). 8vo, original linen-backed boards.

Third (first American) edition. One of 26 lettered copies, specially bound and signed. With the John Kobler bookplate.

The trade style "John Calder Ltd. / London" appears in small type at the foot of the title page. On the verso, Calder is listed as "Foreign Distributor" for Great Britain.

167. *Watt.* London: John Calder (1963). A Jupiter Book. By arrangement with The Olympia Press. 12mo, original wrappers, illustrated with a photographic portrait of Beckett by Sewell. Fourth (first English) edition.

168. "Watt." In *L'Ephémère*, No. 6 (Summer 1968). Small 4to, original pictorial wrappers.

An extract from the French version of *Watt*, which appeared several months before publication of the full text. The passage contains several variants from the first French edition and is illustrated with wash drawings by Bram van Velde.

169. "L'Histoire de Watt." Translated from the English by Ludovic and Agnès Janvier in collaboration with the author. In *Les Lettres Nouvelles* (September–October 1968). 8vo, original printed wrappers.

Extract from Part IV of the French version of *Watt*, first published in its entirety in 1968.

170. *Watt.* Paris: Les Editions de Minuit (1968). Translated from the English by Ludovic and Agnès Janvier in collaboration with the author. Square 12mo, original wrappers, uncut and unopened.

First French edition. One of 90 large-paper copies printed on *Alfamousse.*
Beckett has inscribed this copy on the title page: "for John & Evelyn [Kobler] / with love from Sam / Paris juin 71."

171. Photograph of Samuel Beckett taken by a street photographer outside Burlington House in Piccadilly, ca. 1954.

171

163

COLLECTION MERLIN

1953

is pleased to annouce the publication of

WATT

a novel in English by

SAMUEL BECKETT

The original edition consists of 1,125 copies, the first 25 of which printed on luxury paper signed by the author will be lettered A to Y and will be sold at 2,500 frs, £ 2.10 or $ 7.00. The remaining copies numbered 1 to 1,100 printed on fine paper will be sold at 850 frs, 17/6 or $ 2.50.

Subscription Form

I, _____ , wish

to subscribe to   copies of

WATT, for which I enclose _____ .

Subscriber's address

Les Temps Modernes

1re année   REVUE MENSUELLE   n° 10

1er Juillet 1946

Rédaction, administration : 5, rue Sébastien-Bottin, Paris

172

NOUVELLES ET TEXTES POUR RIEN
STORIES AND TEXTS FOR NOTHING

Along with *Watt* and *Mercier et Camier* (q.v.), one of the more long-drawn-out publishing histories in Beckett's career is that leading up to *Nouvelles et textes pour rien*. "Suite" and the other short stories later collected under that title were among Beckett's first writings in French. But the span from writing to full publication stretched across a full decade that began in the early postwar period.

On 15 December 1946 Beckett wrote to Reavey: "I hope to have a book of short stories ready for the Spring (in French). I do not think I shall write very much in English in the future."

That "book of short stories," plumped out by a group of thirteen shorter texts, became *Nouvelles et textes pour rien* and was not published until 1955. At least part of the reason lies in the fate of Beckett's first published story—"Suite" (see below).

172. "Suite." In *Les Temps Modernes*. Edited by Jean-Paul Sartre. lᵉ année, No. 10 (1 July 1946). 8vo, original printed wrappers, uncut and partly unopened.

> On 27 May 1946 Beckett wrote to George Reavey: "Have finished my French story ["Suite"], about 45:000 words I think. The first half is appearing in the July *Temps Modernes*. . . . I hope to have the complete story published as a separate work. In France they don't bother counting words. Camus's *Etranger* is not any longer." And on 1 September: "The first part of my story *Suite* has appeared in the July number of the *Temps Modernes* and the second and last part will appear in October."
>
> Beckett's expectations for the second half of his long story were frustrated when Simone de Beauvoir, whose word was law in such matters at *Les Temps Modernes*, decided it was somehow not fitting to run it. She claimed that she and Sartre had thought the first half was the whole story, claimed further that the first half was complete in itself and needed no suite. In the following letter, Beckett argued eloquently against the "mutilation" of his story:
>
> > Chère Mme. de Beauvoir,
> >
> > Hier Mme. Clerx m'a appris votre décision au sujet de la 2ᵇᵐᵉ partie de *Suite*.
> >
> > Je regrette ce malentendu qui vous met dans l'obligation d'arrêter ma nouvelle à mi-chemin. C'est un regret de victime.
> >
> > Vous pensez à la bonne tenue de votre revue. Cela est naturel. Moi je pense au personnage de *Suite* frustré de son

repos. Cela aussi est naturel, je pense. Je me mets difficilement à votre place, puisque je ne comprends rien aux questions de rédaction. Mais j'ai lu vos livres, et sais que vous pouvez vous mettre à la mienne.

Je ne voudrais pas que vous vous mépreniez sur le sens de cette lettre, que je n'écris qu'après de longues hésitations. Je n'ai pas envie de discuter. Je ne vous demande pas de revenir sur ce que vous avez décidé. Mais il m'est décidément impossible de me dérober au devoir que je me sens vis-à-vis d'une créature. Pardonnez-moi ces grands mots. Si j'avais peur du ridicule, je me tairais.

J'ai assez confiance en vous, finalement, pour vous dire tout simplement mon sentiment. Le voici. Vous m'accordez la parole pour me la retirer avant qu'elle n'ait eu le temps de rien signifier. Vous immobilisez une existence au seuil de sa solution. Cela a quelque chose de cauchemardesque. J'ai du mal à croire que des soucis de présentation puissent justifier à vos yeux une mutilation pareille.

Vous pensez que le fragment paru dans votre dernier numéro est une chose achevée. Ce n'est pas mon avis. Ce n'est qu'une prémisse majeure.

Ne m'en voulez pas de cette franchise. Elle est sans rancune. Il y a une misère qu'il faut défendre jusqu'au bout, dans le travail et en dehors du travail.

Croyez à mon estime la plus sincère.

[Samuel Beckett]

But Madame de Beauvoir remained unmoved. It was nine years from that point before the full story of "Suite" (in the original French and by then renamed "La Fin") was published.

173. "The End." Translated from the French by Richard Seaver in collaboration with the author. In *Merlin*, Vol. II, No. 3 (Summer-Autumn 1954). 8vo, original green wrappers.

First printing in English and first appearance of Beckett's short story "Suite" in its entirety, published here under a new title, "The End."
Inscribed beneath the title: "translation of *La Fin* (c.f. / *Nouvelles et Textes pour Rien.)* / This story (1945) was first / text written directly in French. / for Jake Schwartz / from Samuel Beckett / Paris Sept. 1957."
Although Beckett is listed here as collaborator, the translation would appear to be Seaver's own, to judge from the account he has given in the introduction to his anthology of Beckett's work, *I Can't Go On, I'll Go On* (New York: Grove Press, 1976), pp. xxiii-xxv. (See No. 379.)

174. "The End." Translated from the French by Richard Seaver in collaboration with the author. In *Evergreen Review*, Vol. IV, No. 15 (November–December 1960). 12mo, original illustrated wrappers.

This version has extensive variants from the translation appearing in

Merlin and would seem to be the one which resulted from the Beckett-Seaver collaboration referred to in No. 173.

Inscribed above the title: "This is the translation of the first story / I wrote in French (1945?), published as / "La Fin" in "Nouvelles et Textes pour Rien." / for Jake Schwartz / Brighton march 1961 / Sam. Beckett."

175. "L'Expulsé." Autograph manuscript, signed, begun 6 October 1946, completed 14 October 1946, 51 pp., small 4to.

Written in ink in a schoolboy's bound notebook, inscribed on the cover, "Samuel Beckett / First published in / *Fontaine* / figures in *Nouvelles / et Textes pour Rien.*" The manuscript has additions, deletions, revisions, and a few decorative doodles, including some in pencil on the front cover.

The first two pages of this notebook are, in fact, the final pages of the autograph manuscript of *Mercier et Camier* (see No. 365). A manuscript page at the end has penciled notes in another hand.

176. "L'Expulsé." In *Fontaine: Revue mensuelle de la poésie et des lettres françaises.* Edited by Max-Pol Fouchet. Vol. X, No. 57 (December 1946–January 1947). 8vo, original printed wrappers, uncut and partly unopened.

First printing.

"L'Expulsé"—"dealing with the same deadbeat as in 'Suite,'" as Beckett described it to George Reavey—is Beckett's world in microcosm and a masterpiece of the short story:

> Je ne sais pas pourquoi j'ai raconté cette histoire. J'aurais pu tout aussi bien en raconter une autre. Peut-être qu'une autre fois je pourrai en raconter une autre. Ames vives, vous verrez que cela se ressemble.

177. "The Expelled." In *Evergreen Review*, Vol. VI, No. 22 (January–February 1962). Translated by Richard Seaver in collaboration with the author. 12mo, original pictorial wrappers. First printing in English.

178. *Der Ausgestossene.* Translated by Elmar Tophoven. With eleven original woodcuts by Roswitha Quadflieg. Hamburg: Raamin-Presse (1976). Small folio, original embossed boards.

German translation of "L'Expulsé."

Limited to 170 copies hand-printed in 10-point Madison-Antiqua. Binding designed by Christian Zwang. This is the author's copy (No. II).

With a presentation inscription signed "Samuel Beckett" on the title page.

179. "Le Calmant." Autograph manuscript, signed, begun 23 December 1946, 76 pp., small-4to notebook.

With deletions, additions, and emendations in ink and in brown

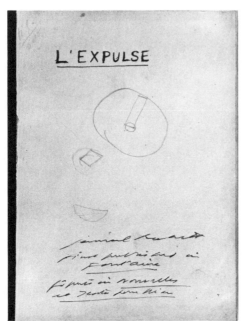

L'EXPULSE

175   178

179

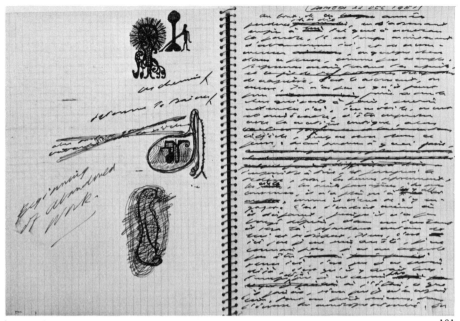

181

crayon, some doodles and sketches, and an arithmetical calculation on the inside front flyleaf. Beckett has signed the front cover and written, *"Le Calmant /* Figures in */ Nouvelles et Textes / pour Rien."*

The last page of text contains lines of dialogue and narrative which appear, in slightly different form, in the full version of "Suite"—"La Fin." Laid in is a 4to sheet of onionskin containing a brief autograph passage intended for insertion in the first of the "Textes pour rien" ("Brusquement, non, à force, à force").

"Le Calmant" wasn't published until 1955, when Les Editions de Minuit brought out *Nouvelles et textes pour rien,* a collection of three short stories and thirteen short prose texts. It first appeared in English in 1967—as "The Calmative"—just prior to Grove Press's edition, *Stories and Texts for Nothing.*

180. "The Calmative." In *Evergreen,* Vol. XI, No. 47 (June 1967). Small folio, original pictorial wrappers.

First printing of this short story in English. Illustrated with reproductions of two of the six drawings by Avigdor Arikha which were added to the second French edition of *Nouvelles et textes pour rien* (1958).

181. "Textes pour rien." Autograph manuscript, signed, 1950–51, 230 pp., including 82 pp. of an abandoned text, in two 4to spiral-bound notebooks.

The manuscript is written in blue and black inks and has numerous deletions and some additions (many of them long) in blue, black, and purple inks. Both notebooks have doodles, usually quite intricate; the second notebook has diagrams, charts, and mathematical calculations as well.

The first notebook contains eight of the thirteen short prose pieces Beckett called "textes pour rien"; (1) "Brusquement, non, à force, à force," begun Christmas Eve 1950; (2) "Là-haut c'est la lumière," begun 4 February 1951, completed 6 February 1951; (3) "Laisse," begun 27 February 1951, completed 5 March 1951; (4) "Où irais-je, si je pouvais aller," begun 10 March 1951, completed 12 March 1951; (5) "Je tiens la greffe," begun 19 March 1951, completed 24 March 1951; (6) "Entre ces apparitions," begun 24 March 1951, completed at Ussy, 28 April 1951; (7) "Ai-je tout essayé," begun in Paris, 5 May 1951, completed 21 May 1951; (8) "Seul les mots rompent le silence," begun in Paris, 25 June 1951, completed 10 July 1951.

The last page of the notebook contains autograph notes in Beckett's hand and one other.

He has written at the bottom of the front cover: "Textes Pr Rien / 1–8 / Ms. original / for / Jake Schwartz / from / Sam. Beckett / Paris Feb. 1960." The alternative titles "Minutes" and "Contes" appear at the top.

The second notebook contains (1) "Si je disais, Là il y a une issue," begun at Ussy 14 July 1951, completed 6 August 1951; (2) "Abandonner, mais c'est tout abandonné," begun 8 August 1951, completed 18 August; (3) "Quand je pense, non, ça ne va pas," begun 20 August 1951, completed at Ussy, 4 September 1951; (4) "Elle faiblit encore," begun in Paris, 7 November 1951, completed 23 November; (5) "C'est une nuit d'hiver," completed 20 December 1951.

On the front cover Beckett has written: "Textes Pr Rien / 9–13 / Ms. original / followed / by abandoned / work. / for / Jake Schwartz / from Sam. Beckett / Paris Feb. 1960."

The "abandoned work"—so marked by Beckett, apparently at a later date, with a different pen—was begun on 22 December 1951 and consists of 82 pages, showing extensive revision and modification. The manuscript has one other intermediate date of composition, 1 February 1952, but no date or indication of completion. There are doodles, sketches for floor plans, and charts interspersed throughout. The last two pages of the notebook have drafts of three letters.

The dates attached to the pieces in the second of these two notebooks, as well as the length of the abandoned work, would suggest that the 82-page fragment was an aborted attempt to move into a longer work immediately upon completion of the "Textes pour rien."

182. "Trois textes pour rien." In *Les Lettres Nouvelles*, 1ᵉ année, No. 3 (May 1953). 8vo, original printed wrappers, uncut and unopened.

The three texts which are printed here correspond to Nos. III ("Laisse"), VI ("Entre ces apparitions"), and X ("Abandonner, mais c'est tout abandonné") of the published version, with variants. Others had appeared in *Arts-Spectacles* (3–9 July 1953) and *Monde Nouveau/Paru* (May–June 1955) prior to their publication in the collected edition *Nouvelles et textes pour rien* (November 1955).

183. *Nouvelles et textes pour rien.* [Paris] Les Editions de Minuit (1955). 8vo, original printed wrappers, uncut and unopened.

First edition.

One of 30 numbered large-paper copies on *pur fil,* of a total edition of 1,185.

Inscribed on the half-title: "for John [Kobler] from Sam / Paris april / 1966."

Included in this collected edition are the short stories "L'Expulsé," "Le Calmant" (published here for the first time in French), "La Fin" (first appearance in French of the complete story "Suite"), and the thirteen short prose works "Textes pour rien," numbered I–XIII.

184. _____. Another copy, one of 50 numbered copies, *hors commerce,* on *vélin.*

Review copy, inscribed on the half-title: "pour / George Slocombe / Hommages de l'auteur / Samuel Beckett / Paris nov. 1953 [1955]."

George Slocombe, a writer and journalist from Bristol, England, had a distinguished career as war correspondent and foreign-affairs commentator. In addition, he was the author of novels, books of verse, historical studies, and books about art. At the time *Nouvelles et textes pour rien* was published, he was serving as art critic of the *Paris Herald-Tribune,* for which he wrote also occasional book reviews.

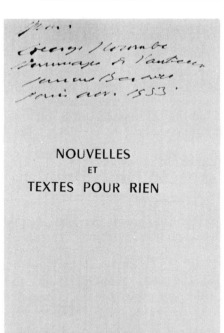

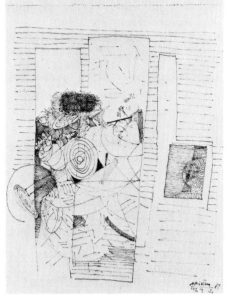

184

185

185. *Nouvelles et textes pour rien.* [Paris] Les Editions de Minuit (1958). 8vo, original wrappers, illustrated with a drawing by Avigdor Arikha, uncut and partly unopened.

   Second edition, limited to 2,000 copies on *vélin.* Includes reproductions of six drawings by Arikha.
   Inscribed on the half-title: "for / Jake Schwartz / from Sam. Beckett / with best wishes / Paris august 1957 [1958]."

186. _____. Another copy, with a presentation inscription from the artist to the Koblers on the illustration facing the title page.

187. "Der erste der 'Textes pour Rien.'" In *Texte und Zeichen: Eine literarische Zeitschrift,* 3rd year, No. 14 (1957). 8vo, original wrappers. First printing in German of No. I of the "Textes pour rien."

188. *Erzählungen und Texte um Nichts.* Translated from the French by Elmar Tophoven. [Frankfurt am Main] Suhrkamp Verlag (1962). 12mo, original boards, dust jacket. First German edition, which preceded the first publication in English.

189. "Text for Nothing I." Translated from the French by the author. In *Evergreen Review,* Vol. III, No. 9 (Summer 1959). 8vo, original pictorial wrappers. First printing in English.

190. *Stories and Texts for Nothing.* New York: Grove Press (1967). 8vo, original cloth, dust jacket, back cover illustrated with a portrait of Beckett by Arikha.

   First edition in English of *Nouvelles et textes pour rien.* With reproductions of the six drawings by Avigdor Arikha used in the second French edition.
   Inscribed by the artist, in pencil, on the frontispiece: "For John and Evelyn [Kobler], in / friendship from / Avigdor / N.Y. March 1967."

191. "Texts for Nothing XII." In *The Transatlantic Review,* No. 24 (Spring 1967). 8vo, original printed wrappers. An English prepublication appearance.

192. "Texts for Nothing: VI." In *The London Magazine,* Vol. VII, No. 5, New Series (August 1967). 8vo, original pictorial wrappers. An English prepublication appearance.

193. *No's Knife. Collected Shorter Prose. 1945–1966.* London: Calder and Boyars (1967). 8vo, full calf, gilt fillet, all edges gilt. In publisher's slipcase.

   One of an edition of 100 numbered copies "printed A *(hors commerce)*" and signed by the author. The limitation page states that these copies were "bound in quarter calf and buckram," but as described above, this one is bound in full calf.
   Like the Grove Press edition, this first English collected edition

contains Beckett's short stories and "Texts for Nothing" and includes, in addition, "From an Abandoned Work," "Imagination Dead Imagine," "Enough," and "Ping," the latter two appearing here for the first time in book form.

194. _____. Another copy, one of "a second series of 100 numbered copies printed B and signed by the author *(hors commerce)*." The limitation page indicates that this series was to be "bound in full buckram," but this copy, at least, is bound in "quarter" calf, all edges gilt, in publisher's cloth slipcase.

   Inscribed on the title page: "for / John & Evelyn [Kobler] / with love from Sam / Paris nov. 67."

195. Documents relating to *Nouvelles et textes pour rien:*

   Two typed letters, signed, from David Solomon, assistant editor of *Esquire: The Magazine for Men*, to George Reavey, dated 19 November 1958 and 12 February 1959 and 1 typed note, "Dave" [Solomon] to George [Reavey]. With manuscript notes in Reavey's hand.
   When *Esquire* expressed interest in publishing a work of Beckett's, Reavey lent David Solomon his inscribed copy of *Nouvelles et textes pour rien*. Solomon found the first *texte pour rien* "of particular interest," but said they would be happy if Beckett would give them *"any* translation of *any* of his short stories," not yet published in English.
   The publisher, however, took a different view. In a follow-up note to his 12-February letter, Solomon told Reavey that [Arnold Gingrich] had characterized the book as the "'dreariest of dreary existentialism.'"

196. Samuel Beckett with his German publisher, Siegfried Unseld, Stuttgart, ca. 1978.

197. Jean Wahl. "The Word is Graven." In *Illustrations for the Bible* by Marc Chagall. With an appreciation by Meyer Schapiro. New York: Harcourt, Brace and Company (1956). Folio, original color-illustrated boards.

   Printed beneath Jean Wahl's name, at the end of the poem, is the acknowledgment: "The poems have been translated from the french original by / the author with the kind assistance of Samuel BECKET [*sic*]."
   The edition contains reproductions of 105 etchings by Chagall, printed by Draeger Frères. In addition, sixteen original lithographs in color and twelve in black, as well as the cover and the title page, were composed specially for this work and printed by Mourlot Frères.
   This book, in its original French edition, constitutes a double number (33–34) of the deluxe art review *Verve*.

198. "From an Abandoned Work." Autograph manuscript, signed, 1958, 22 pp. in two gatherings of sheets sewn separately and marked I and II, small 4to.

On 15 March 1958 Samuel Beckett wrote to Jake Schwartz, "I have had a sharp spell of work and have not yet transcribed for you *From An Abandoned Work*. But I have not forgotten and shall do so on my return next week to the country." He was as good as his word and this manuscript is the result. It has a number of omissions, vis-à-vis the published text, and is inscribed on the last page: "[This text was written 1954 or / 1955. / It is the first text written directly / in English since *Watt (1945)*. / Above transcription made March / 1958 for my friend / Jake Schwartz] / Sam. Beckett." On the first page Beckett has written, "Transcript of *From an Abandoned Work*." First publication of the work was entrusted—abandoned—to *Trinity News: A Dublin University Weekly* (7 June 1956), whose student editors edited Beckett's text to a fare-thee-well, "improving" his punctuation and tidying up in general. Needless to say, he was not amused.

The piece was broadcast by the BBC's Third Programme, on 14 December 1957, in a reading by Patrick Magee, produced by Donald McWhinnie.

195   196

90

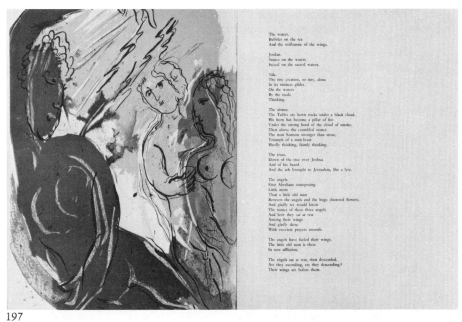

The waters.
Bubbles on the sea
And the oriflamme of the wings.

Jordan.
Stones on the waters
Sacred on the sacred waters.

Nile.
The tiny creature, so tiny, alone
In its tininess glides
On the waters
By the reeds
Thinking.

The stones.
The Tables are hewn rocks under a black cloud.
His horn has become a pillar of fire
Under the strong hand of the cloud of smoke.
Then above the crumbled stones
The man Samson stronger than stone.
Triumph of a man-beast
Hardly thinking, faintly thinking.

The trees.
Down of the tree over Joshua
And of his beard
And the ark brought to Jerusalem, like a lyre.

The angels.
First Abraham unimposing
Little more
Than a little old man
Between the angels and the huge clustered flowers.
And gladly we would know
The names of these three angels
And how they sat at rest
Among their wings
And gladly these
With sweetest prayers smooth.

The angels have furled their wings.
The little old man is there
In sore affliction.

The angels sat at rest, then descended.
Are they ascending, are they descending?
Their wings are before them.

197

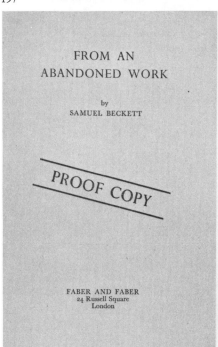

FROM AN
ABANDONED WORK

by
SAMUEL BECKETT

PROOF COPY

FABER AND FABER
24 Russell Square
London

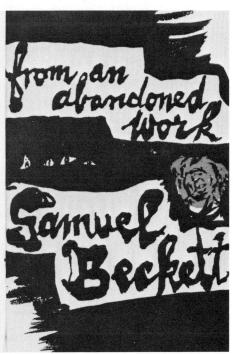

200   201

199. "From an Abandoned Work." In *Evergreen Review*, Vol. I, No. 3 (1957). 8vo, original pictorial wrappers.

> First printing.
> Inscribed on the half-title: "for Jake Schwartz / from Sam. Beckett / Paris March 1958."

200. *From an Abandoned Work*. London: Faber and Faber (1958). 8vo, original orange printed wrappers. Proof copy of the first edition, inscribed by Samuel Beckett on the title page.

201. *From an Abandoned Work*. London: Faber and Faber (1958). 8vo, original pictorial wrappers.

> First edition.
> Inscribed on the title page: "for / John Kobler / with all good wishes from / Sam. Beckett / Paris jan. 1965."

From an Abandoned Work. See also Nos. 193, 352, 353, 363.

202. *D'un ouvrage abandonné*. Translated from the English by Ludovic and Agnès Janvier in collaboration with the author. [Paris] Les Editions de Minuit (1967). 12mo, original printed wrappers, uncut and unopened.

> One of 222 numbered large-paper copies on *vélin cuve B.F.K. Rives*.
> Inscribed on the half-title: "for / John & Evelyn [Kobler] / with love from Sam / Paris march / 1967."

ALL THAT FALL
TOUS CEUX QUI TOMBENT

In a letter to Nancy Cunard, dated 4 July 1956, Beckett wrote: "Saw Barry of BBC TV who is interested in the mime [*Act Without Words*] (and why not?) and am told Gielgud wants a play for 3rd Programme. Never thought about Radio play technique but in the dead of t'other night got a nice gruesome idea full of cartwheels and dragging of feet and puffing and panting which may or may not lead to something." It did "lead to something"— Beckett's first radio play, *All That Fall*.

Several months later he wrote to Nancy Cunard again: "Am just finishing a script for the Third, request performance, but which will probably never see the air. Queer to be struggling with English again." But the struggle was not in vain, and on 7 November he wrote her: "The 3rd have taken the radio script for broadcast to the 4 winds in January."

All That Fall was broadcast in the BBC Third Programme on 13 January 1957, produced by Donald McWhinnie. The cast included two of Beckett's favorite actors—Patrick Magee as Mr. Slocum and Jack MacGowran as Tommy.

203. "All That Fall." Autograph manuscript, signed [1956], 68 pp., of which 63 are in Beckett's hand, small 4to, full crimson morocco, gilt fillets.

   The original title, "Lovely Day for the Races," has been crossed out and replaced by "All That Fall." The manuscript, written in blue, black, and red ink, has numerous deletions, revisions, and additions, some doodles, mathematical calculations, and word lists (crossed out). On the last page of the manuscript, Beckett has written the date of completion, "Ussy September 1956"; on the title page, "for Jake Schwartz / with best wishes / for 1957 / Samuel Beckett / Paris / January 1957."

204. "All That Fall." Carbon copy of typed manuscript, signed [1956], 27 pp., 4to, crimson morocco-backed cloth.

   With some corrections and a few deletions and additions. Beckett has written "All That Fall / Original Typescript" above the cast of characters and, below, "Samuel Beckett / Paris 1956." A review of the first BBC broadcast of the play, from the 24 January 1957 issue of *The Listener*, is pasted on the facing flyleaf.

205. *All That Fall / Tous ceux qui tombent*. Produced by Donald McWhinnie. BBC Third Programme, 13 January 1957. Folio, original wrappers, spiral binding.

   The BBC entered (unsuccessfully) Beckett's first radio play, *All That*

Fall, for the Italia Prize of 1957. Two and a half years later, the prize was given to Beckett's play *Embers*. The French version of *All That Fall—Tous ceux qui tombent*—accompanies the English text.

206. *All That Fall*. New York: Grove Press (1957). 8vo, original cloth-backed boards. First edition in English. One of "a specially bound, limited edition of 100 numbered copies."

207. *All That Fall*. New York: Grove Press (1957). 8vo, original cloth.

     First edition in English, regular issue.
     Inscribed on the title page: "for / Jake Schwartz / with best wishes / Sam. Beckett / Paris Sept. 1957."

208. *All That Fall: A Play*. London: Faber and Faber (1957). 8vo, original wrappers.

     Proof copy of the first English edition.
     Inscribed on the flyleaf: "for / John and Evelyn [Kobler] / affection-ately / Sam / Ussy April 69."
     There are a few minor stylistic differences in the *mise en pages* between the proof and the printed edition. The subtitle for the printed edition is more specific—"A Play for Radio."

209. *All That Fall. A Play for Radio*. London: Faber and Faber (1957). 8vo, original pictorial wrappers.

     First English edition.
     Inscribed on the title page: "First produced on / BBC 3rd Programme / January 13th 1957 / Producer: / Donald McWhinnie / With best wishes / for Jake Schwartz / Sam. Beckett / Paris Sept. 1957."

     All That Fall. See also No. 263.

210. "Tous ceux qui tombent (Texte Radiophonique)." In *Les Lettres Nouvelles*, 5ᵉ année, No. 47 (March 1957). Crown 8vo, original printed wrappers, uncut and unopened.

     Signed by Beckett on the first page of the play, beneath his printed name.
     First appearance of this radio play in French. Translation by Robert Pinget (see No. 270).

211. *Tous ceux qui tombent. Pièce radiophonique*. Translated from the English by Robert Pinget. [Paris] Les Editions de Minuit (1957). 8vo, original wrappers, uncut and unopened.

     First edition of the French translation. One of 80 numbered copies on *pur fil Marais*.
     Inscribed on the flyleaf: "for / John & Evelyn [Kobler] / with love from Sam / Paris May 67."

212. *Tous ceux qui tombent. Pièce radiophonique.* Translated from the English by Robert Pinget. [Paris] Les Editions de Minuit (1957). 8vo, original wrappers, uncut and unopened.

First French edition, regular issue.
With a presentation inscription on the front cover from Beckett to Jake [Schwartz].

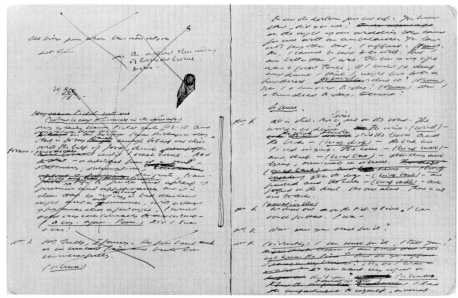

203

8th January 1958.

Dear Mr Devine,

"End-Game"

I write in reply to your letter of January 7th, in which you say that Mr Beckett feels that he cannot make an alteration to the passage on page 28.

In the circumstances the Lord Chamberlain will not be able to grant a Licence for the public performance of this Play.

Yours sincerely,

G.Devine Esq.

See page 97

FIN DE PARTIE / ACTE SANS PAROLES
ENDGAME / ACT WITHOUT WORDS

Where to, after *Godot?* Onward and upward, *comme sur des roulettes*, one might have thought. Not so. The new play, *Fin de partie*—"more inhuman," Beckett called it—brought a long series of problems of all kinds. First, he was "very dissatisfied with it," as he wrote to Susan Manning on 15 March 1956. Then in November, George Devine, director of the Royal Court Theatre in London, enlisted the help of Eugène Ionesco in an attempt to secure the English rights to *Fin de partie* and also to arrange a performance of Beckett's mime, *Acte sans paroles*, in tandem with Ionesco's *Les Chaises*. Beckett told Devine there was "little possibility of my undertaking the translation for some considerable time. I am not even sure that an English version is possible." He wrote to Susan Manning: "I am so tired of translations and bad productions abroad and misunderstanding all round that my feeling is to leave [it] in French for some time at least. . . . It is a difficult unpleasant work and I cannot see it in English."

There was some discussion about presenting *Fin de partie* with *Les Chaises*, but on reflection Beckett decided *Fin de partie* was too long—over an hour and a half at that time—to fit into such an arrangement, and he suggested that the Royal Court Theatre couple *Acte sans paroles* with *Les Chaises* and add another short piece by Ionesco or perhaps use "one of Yeats's [Four] *Plays for Dancers* ?—[At] *The Hawk's Well*, for example, where there is so much great poetry."

For his part, Devine found *Acte sans paroles* "wonderful, poetic, comic and theatrical" but decided, after all, "it doesn't belong with *Les Chaises*." Why not do it with *Fin de partie* —in French? All along, Beckett had wanted *Fin de Partie* and *Acte sans paroles* (with music by his cousin John Beckett, written for the dancer Deryk Mendel) to open in Paris. And so he kept turning aside Devine's request to put on *Fin de partie* in French and began to work on a translation with the understanding that the Royal Court Theatre would not perform it in English before its premiere in French, in Paris.

Earlier there had been talk of presenting "the one-act horror," as he referred to *Fin de partie* in a 6-June letter to Nancy Cunard, at the Marseilles Festival, but Beckett really preferred, as he wrote to Susan Manning, to "keep it for a Paris theatre." And in the end he missed the Marseilles deadline—deliberately, it would appear: "Impossible to get anything definite out of the organizers, no contracts for actors, no information about theatre and equipment, so rather than have the play bungled I think we shall withdraw it," he wrote to Nancy Cunard soon after.

Several Paris theaters showed interest and then backed away, including the Théâtre de l'Oeuvre, where Lugné-Poë had mounted his historic production of *Ubu Roi*. Others were greedy. In October Beckett wrote again to Cunard: ". . . You have to go waving million franc notes which we wouldn't even if we could. However we'll find a barn somewhere some day."

He continued to have trouble with his translation—"a hopeless undertaking." Finally, with pressure from all sides, he agreed to let a French company, led by Roger Blin, put on the play in French at the Royal Court. But with that settled, his troubles had just begun. Mrs. Grundy, in the form of the Lord Chamberlain—Lord Scarborough—was still in office. A copy of the play was dispatched to "His Nibs," accompanied by the two-guinea Reading Fee and the five-shilling stamping charge, with a plea for a hasty decision. In five days, there were rumblings of discontent with some of the "sex slang." The Lord Chamberlain suggested Beckett substitute *"bêtises"* for *"conneries."* Beckett countered with *"âneries."* The Lord Chamberlain agreed. In short order the license was granted, and soon amended, on request, to include *Acte sans paroles.* On 3 April the two were performed at the Royal Court Theatre. "Rather an aberration. There wasn't much sense," Beckett wrote to Mary Manning Howe on 28 April, "playing before people who don't know the language"—ninety percent of them, he said in a letter to Susan Manning—"but we are beginning now in the little Studio des Champs-Elysées [in Paris], with better prospects."

Beckett finished his translation ("well down to my expectations") by August, in spite of "chronic tiredness and horror of pen, ink, and paper," he wrote to George Devine on 13 June. But a problem arose about the curtain-raiser. Devine didn't want the mime (*Act Without Words*) in the English-language production—*Endgame*—because it had already been seen with the French *Fin de partie.* He suggested *All That Fall.* Beckett vetoed that as not adaptable to the stage. Another suggestion proved unacceptable and so Beckett then began work on *Krapp's Last Tape* to accompany *Endgame.*

The final version of *Endgame* reached the Lord Chamberlain's Office just before Christmas 1957 and then the struggle began in earnest. "Balls" and "arses" were frowned upon, as was the line "I'd like to pee." The worst affront to his Lordship, however, was the passage beginning with "Let us pray to God," and ending, two pages further along, with "The bastard! He doesn't exist." Devine suggested either a club production or (half-facetiously) performing the offending lines in French, since he already had a license for the French text. The day after Christmas, Beckett sent acceptable substitutes for everything except the prayer passage. And there, he drew the line. "I am afraid I simply cannot accept omission or modification of the prayer passage, which appears to me indispensable as it stands," he wrote to Devine. "And to play it in French would amount to an omission, for nine tenths of the audience. I think this does call for a firm stand. It is no more blasphemous than 'My God, my God, why hast Thou forsaken me?'" Ten days later he wrote, "I have shown that I am prepared to put up with minor damage which God knows is bad enough in this kind of fragile writing. But no author can acquiesce in what he considers, rightly or wrongly, as grave injury to his work.

"I am extremely sorry to have to take this stand and I can assure you I do not do so lightly."

Three days later the Lord Chamberlain refused a license for *Endgame.* Devine arranged a private reading of the play for His Lordship's advisers; from that it emerged that the immovable roadblock was the play's reference to "The Almighty" as a "bastard." Devine asked Beckett for a gentler term. Beckett suggested "swine." After further negotiations, conciliatory noises began to be heard in the corridors of power. Beckett was asked for three other choices of equal "virulence." On 28 July 1958, he wrote that he was "tired . . . of all this buggering around with guardsmen, riflemen, and hussars. There are no alternatives to 'bastard' agreeable to me. Nevertheless I have offered them 'swine' in its place. This is definitely and finally as far as I'll go. . . . If 'swine' is not acceptable, then there is nothing left but to have a club production or else call the whole thing off. I simply refuse to play along any further with these licensing grocers.

"I should like to assure you, whatever course you adopt, and to mark in a small way my gratitude to you personally and to the Royal Court Theatre, that I undertake here and now to offer you the first option on UK rights of my next play, in the unlikely event of my ever writing another."

On 6 August a license was issued for "End Game" [*sic*] by the Lord Chamberlain's Office. A week later Beckett wrote to Mary Manning Howe, "I had a letter from Devine yesterday with the captivating news that the LC has accepted 'swine' in the place of 'bastard' and is licensing the play's public performance. There's a nicety of blasphemy for you."

A perfunctory and anticlimactic rear-guard skirmish took place over the script of *Krapp's Last Tape.* The Lord Chamberlain eventually withdrew his objections, a license was granted on 10 October, and on the 28th, *Endgame* and *Krapp's Last Tape* were given their world premiere.

213. *Fin de partie suivi de Acte sans paroles.* [Paris] Les Editions de Minuit (1957). 8vo, original wrappers, uncut and unopened.

    First edition. Large-paper copy, one of 50 on *vélin pur fil du Marais.* Inscribed on the title page: "for John [Kobler] / from Sam / Paris April / 1966."
    The play was written especially for Roger Blin and is dedicated to him.

214. *Fin de partie suivi de Acte sans paroles.* [Paris] Les Editions de Minuit (1957). 8vo, original wrappers, uncut and unopened.

    First edition, regular issue.
    Inscribed on the half-title: "for / Jake Schwartz / in friendship / Sam. Beckett / Paris february 1957."

Fin de partie. See also No. 263.

Acte sans paroles. See also Nos. 238, 263.

for
Jake Schwartz
in friendship
Sam. Beckett
Paris february 1957

Fin de partie

ENDGAME

A Play in One Act

followed by

ACT WITHOUT WORDS
A Mime for One Player

by

Samuel Beckett

to Jane & Evelyn
affectionately
Sam
one april 1958

translated from the French
by the author

Hope is a thread that tells us moments
which till I take no happiness that might
I take from Hell's and write on hell at war
All hope abandon ye who enter in .

(Inscribed to Chamfort)

Grove Press, Inc.   **New York**

214 218

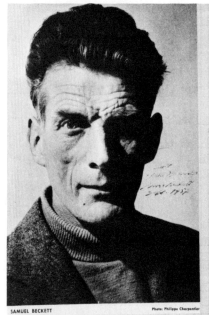

SAMUEL BECKETT   Photo: Philippe Charpentier

215

100

215. "Endgame." Autograph manuscript, signed, 106 pp., begun in Paris on 7 May 1957, completed at Ussy on 5 June 1957, written in blue, black, and purple inks in small-4to cloth-backed notebook.

Lightly revised; some doodles.

The cover of the notebook has the title *All That Fall* crossed out. (Beckett had been working on *All That Fall* as he was finishing *Fin de partie*.) On the inside flyleaf Beckett has written: "This is the original MS of / my translation of Fin de / Partie. / Samuel Beckett / commenced May 1957 / finished June 1957 / created in French in / London, at the Royal / Court Theatre, April 1957." Laid in is a reproduction of a photograph of Samuel Beckett by Philippe Charpentier, pasted onto a loose sheet from the notebook and inscribed: "for / Jake Schwartz / Sam. Beckett / Sept. 1957."

216. "Act Without Words. (Acte sans paroles)." Autograph manuscript, signed, 4 pp., on two loose sheets from an exercise notebook, small 4to.

With minor variants from the printed text. An autograph note on page 4 reads: "Translated from original French by / the author. / For Jake Schwartz, with / best wishes. / Xmas 1957. / Samuel Beckett."

Beckett wrote the mime *Act Without Words* originally in French as a companion piece to *Fin de partie*. But although he dropped it, in favor of *Krapp's Last Tape*, for the Royal Court's production of *Endgame*, the mime accompanies *Endgame* in both the French and English editions of the play.

Act Without Words. See also Nos. 262, 352, 353.

217. *Endgame: A Play in One Act followed by Act Without Words: A Mime for One Player.* Translated from the French by the author. New York: Grove Press (1958). 12mo, original cloth-backed boards.

First edition in English. One of a specially bound, limited edition of 100 numbered copies.

The English text varies from the French: Clov's song has been cut out and the passage where Clov spots the little boy from the window has been greatly reduced.

218. *Endgame: A Play in One Act Followed by Act Without Words: A Mime for One Player.* Translated from the French by the author. New York: Grove Press (1958). 8vo, original pictorial wrappers.

Inscribed on the title page, "for John and Evelyn [Kobler] / affectionately / Sam / Ussy April 1969," followed by:

Hope is a fraud that fools us evermore
Which till I lost no happiness was mine
I take from Hell's and write on Heaven's door
All hope abandon ye who enter in.

(Apologies to Chamfort)

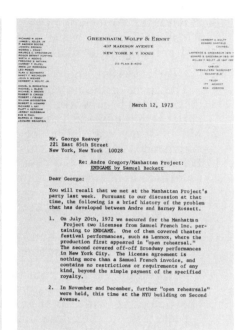

219   223

Four years later, in the Centenary Number of *Hermathena: A Dublin University Review*, Beckett published a revised edition of this quatrain. (See No. 255.)

219. *Endgame: A Play in One Act Followed by Act Without Words: A Mime for One Player.* Translated from the original French by the author. London: Faber and Faber (1958). 8vo, original cloth.

First English edition.
Inscribed on the title page: "for Jake [Schwartz] / from his friend / Sam / Paris May 1958."
A copy of the original London playbill is laid in.

220. _____. Another copy, with original illustrated dust jacket. Signed by Beckett on the title page.

221. *Endspiel (Fin de Partie).* Followed by *Akt ohne Worte (Acte sans paroles).* Translated into German by Elmar Tophoven. Frankfurt am Main: S. Fischer Verlag. Oblong 8vo, original orange wrappers.

Advance copy, in mimeographed form, of the acting edition.
Inscribed on the cover: "for / Jake Schwartz / from his friend / Sam. Beckett / (advance copy)."

222. *Endspiel—Fin de partie.* [Frankfurt am Main] Suhrkamp Verlag (1960). 12mo, original illustrated wrappers.

Bilingual edition.
Inscribed on the title page: "for John & Evelyn [Kobler] / with love from Sam / Paris April 1971."

224

225a

103

223. Jeremy Nussbaum, for Greenbaum, Woolf & Ernst. Typed letter, signed, to George Reavey, 12 March 1973, 5 pp., with photocopies of two typed letters, signed, from Robert P. Levine, for Hellerstein, Rosier & Rembar, to André Gregory and Billy Rose Foundation, 7 and 13 February 1973, 2 pp.

André Gregory's acting company, "Manhattan Project," applied for and received (on 20 July 1972) licenses from Samuel French, Inc., to produce *Endgame* for both theater-festival performances at Lennox, in the Berkshires, and off-off Broadway. The strange chicken-wire set, added dialogue, and other departures from Beckett's concept caused Barney Rosset, Beckett's American publisher, to demand, through his lawyers, that this "distorted version" of *Endgame* be closed down on the grounds that it "contains material and music that destroy the intent and character of the original play."

Mr. Nussbaum's detailed reply gives a step-by-step account of the expression of differences by the two parties—including threats that came to nothing: ". . . it would be most helpful if the situation could be explained to Mr. Beckett, with particular emphasis on how the erstwhile foe of censorship, Mr. Rossett [sic], has strayed from those principles he claimed to take so seriously."

The reviews of the Manhattan Project production ranged from "I love it" (Clive Barnes) to "loose, inventive only at a rather childish level, seriously interruptive (Beckett's own rhythms are destroyed) and, I would say, impertinent" (Walter Kerr).

Although Beckett disapproved of the "distorted version," he decided, in view of the cost and effort that had gone into it, to let it continue for the period for which it had been licensed.

224. Photograph of Alan Schneider rehearsing *Endgame* for the 1958 Cherry Lane production, with Alvin Epstein as Clov, Nydia Westman as Nell, P. J. Kelly as Nagg, and Boris Tumarin in the role (Hamm) created by Lester Rawlins; together with a playbill.

225. Photograph by Gjon Mili of Lester Rawlins as Hamm and Alvin Epstein as Clov in *Endgame* at the Cherry Lane Theatre, 1958.

225a. Photograph of Hume Cronyn in *Act Without Words*, performed for the Samuel Beckett Festival which opened on 20 November 1972 in The Forum Theater at Lincoln Center.

KRAPP'S LAST TAPE
LA DERNIÈRE BANDE

The four heavily corrected typescripts of *Krapp's Last Tape* are a fascinating example of the creative process. The finished play is an eminently poetic work, and these four much-revised preliminary versions reveal Beckett's path in reaching his destination. Typescript I contains the kernel of the idea; sentences are less carefully crafted, some of them still present even two revisions later. In Typescript II there is an expansion of the basic idea, along with the introduction of new material—e.g., the scene with Krapp and the banana—and sentence structure is tightened up. In Typescripts III and IV there is, progressively, further refinement with additional changes to enhance such distinctively Beckettian characteristics as poetic phrasing (in its broader sense: modulation, pace, rhythm), unusual word choice, suggestive ellipsis, and two-edged humor.

226. Untitled ["Krapp's Last Tape"]. Typed manuscript, signed, March 1958, 4 pp., 4to.

Typescript I. With numerous autograph revisions and additions in black ink. There are a few doodles.

The text varies considerably from the published version and lacks, in particular, the introductory stage directions and description of the setting. The protagonist appears as "A."

At the top of page 1 Beckett has written: "Typescript I of *Krapp's Last Tape* 3.58." Inscribed, in blue ink, at the bottom of page 4: "for / Jake Schwartz / Sam. Beckett / March 1958."

227. "Crapp's Last Tape." Typed manuscript, signed, March 1958, 10 pp., 4to.

With many autograph corrections, annotations, and revisions in black and blue inks.

This manuscript, labeled by Beckett as "Typescript II," reflects the changes made in the first typescript (some of which have been revised again) and is a major expansion of that verison, corresponding more recognizably to the published text. Introductory material relating to the stage setting has been added, and the verso of page 1 has a long autograph addition which incorporates stage directions concerning A's [Krapp's] movements. Whereas the first typescript was untitled, here Beckett has written "Crapp's Last Tape" at the top of page 1. A mathematical calculation on the verso of the final page relates to the passage: "To drink less, in particular. And the resolutions! (*Brief laugh of A alone*). Statistics. Seventeen hundred hours, out of the preceding eight thousand odd, consumed on licensed premises alone. Over 20%."

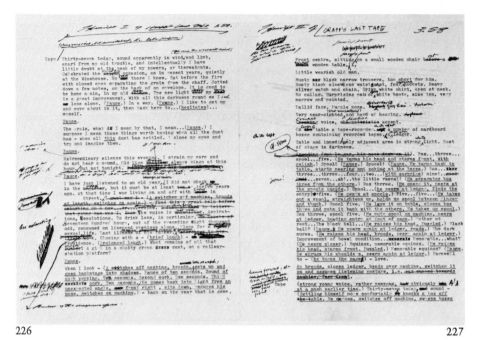

228. "Krapp's Last Tape." Typed manuscript, signed, March 1958, 9 pp., 4to.

"Typescript III," so described in Beckett's hand at the top of the first page. With many autograph emendations and additions, a few doodles, and one mathematical calculation on the verso of the last page. The title now takes its published form and has been typed in (apparently later) at the beginning of the text. Beckett has added a few more details concerning the setting: e.g., "April 1986" has been changed to "a late evening in the nineteen eighties."

Inscribed, in blue ink, on the last page: "for Jake Schwartz / Sam. Beckett / March 1958."

229. "Krapp's Last Tape (Reel)." Typed manuscript, signed, 9 pp., 4to.

This fourth typescript shows a moderate number of corrections and additions in Beckett's hand. The verso of page 5 has an arithmetical computation, not incorporated into the text. Beckett has slightly modified the title, adding "Reel," within parentheses, as a possible alternative for "Tape." Except for a few minor variants, the manuscript is close to the published text.

An authograph note on the final page reads: "Note on technique of tape-recorder." Inscribed: "for / Jake Schwartz / Sam. Beckett / March 1958."

230. "Krapp's Last Tape." Thermofax copy of typed manuscript, 8 pp., 4to.

A still later version. With a few changes and insertions. The title is now definitely "Krapp's Last Tape." Beckett has modified the time from "the nineteen eighties" to "the future."

231. "Krapp's Last Tape." In *Evergreen Review*, Vol. II, No. 5 (Summer 1958). 8vo, original pictorial wrappers.

First printing.
On page 13 Beckett has written in the margin: "Sam. Beckett / First printing (I think) / of this work / March 1961."

232. *Krapp's Last Tape and Embers.* Corrected page proofs. London: Faber and Faber (1959). 8vo, loose in sheets, uncut.

Inscribed on the title page: "corrected proof / for / Jake Schwartz / from / Sam. Beckett / Paris Feb. 1960."

233. *Krapp's Last Tape and Embers.* London: Faber and Faber (1959). 8vo, original green printed wrappers, uncut.

First English edition.
Inscribed on the title page: "for John [Kobler] / from Sam / Paris April / 1966."

Krapp's Last Tape. See also No. 263.

234. "La Dernière bande." Carbon copy of typed manuscript, signed, 9 pp., 4to.

With a few corrections and additions in red and blue inks and in pencil.
Inscribed at top of the first page: "Corrected typescript of / French translation of / 'Krapp's Last Tape' for / Jake Schwartz."

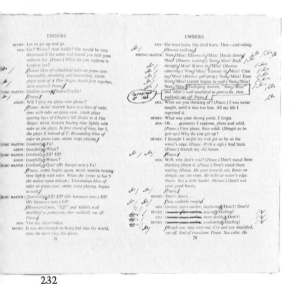

232

233

235. "La Dernière bande (Krapp's Last Tape)." In *Les Lettres Nouvelles,* 7ᵉ année, Nouvelle Série, No. 1 (4 March 1959). Crown 8vo, original printed wrappers.

> Inscribed by Samuel Beckett above the title of the play: "for Jake [Schwartz] from Sam B. / Brighton 1961 / First printing of French translation / Krapp's Last Tape."
> *La Dernière bande* was first performed in Paris at the Théâtre Récamier, along with Pinget's *La Manivelle,* the text of which Beckett had translated as *The Old Tune.* (See Nos. 270-72).

236. *La Dernière bande suivi de Cendres.* Translated from the English by Pierre Leyris and the author. [Paris] Les Editions de Minuit [1960]. 12mo, original wrappers, uncut and unopened.

> First edition in French.
> Inscribed on the half-title: "for / Jake [Schwartz] / from / Sam / Paris 1960."
> Laid in is a printed card explaining that the second play, *Cendres,* is "une pièce radiophonique."

237. *La Dernière bande.* With Robert Pinget's *Lettre Morte.* Illustrated with photographs of the two productions by Agnès Varda. [Paris] Les Editions de Minuit [1960]. 12mo, original printed wrappers.

> Beckett's autograph signature appears under his printed name on the second title page.
> This edition is one of a series "Collection du Répertoire"—plays produced by Jean Vilar for the Théâtre National Populaire. The TNP created *La Dernière bande* at the Théâtre Récamier, with R.-J. Chauffard in the role of Krapp, directed by Roger Blin, on 22 March 1960.

238. *La Dernière bande. Acte sans paroles.* Original illustrated wrappers [Paris, 1970].

> Theater program, with texts by Jean-Louis Barrault, Paul-Louis Mignon, and Ludovic Janvier.
> The Madeleine Renaud—Jean-Louis Barrault company reopened the Théâtre Récamier in February 1970 with a cycle of Samuel Beckett plays. In addition to *Krapp's Last Tape* and *Act Without Words,* they staged *Oh les beaux jours (Happy Days),* with Madeleine Renaud, and a twenty-performance run of *En attendant Godot.*

239. *Krapps sista band.* Translated into Swedish by Lars Kleberg. In *Pegasen 1959.* Uppsala, 1959. Crown 8vo, original decorative wrappers.

> First Swedish edition.
> Inscribed on the inside front cover: "*Krapp* / 1st publication / in Sweden / for Jake [Schwartz] from Sam / Paris 1960."

240

241a   242

FRANCISCO DE TERRAZAS

SONNET

I dreamed that I was thrown from a crag
by one who held my will in servitude,
and all but fallen to the griping jaws
of a wild beast in wait for me below.

In terror, gropingly, I cast around
for wherewith to uphold me with my hands,
and the one closed about a trenchant sword,
and the other twined about a little herb.

Little and little the herb came swift away,
and the sword ever sorer vexed my hand
as I more fiercely clutched its cruel edges...

Oh wretched me, and how from self estranged,
that I rejoice to see me mangled thus
for dread of ending, dying, my distress!

240. *Krapp ou La Dernière bande. Opéra.* Text by Samuel Beckett. Score by Marcel Mihalovici. Paris: Heugel & Cie [1961]. Folio, original pictorial wrappers.

Marcel Mihalovici approached Beckett to write a libretto for an opera commissioned by the Bielefeld Opera Company. Beckett, having an aversion to writing "on command," persuaded him to use one of his works already in existence. Mihalovici's choice was *Krapp's Last Tape.*

241. Photograph of Donald Davis playing in *Krapp's Last Tape,* on a twin bill with Edward Albee's *The Zoo Story* at the Provincetown Playhouse, New York, 1960. With a playbill from the production.

241a. Hume Cronyn in *Krapp's Last Tape,* one of the three plays presented at the Samuel Beckett Festival which opened 20 November 1972 in The Forum Theater at Lincoln Center.

242. ["Anthology of Mexican Poetry"]. Carbon copy of typed manuscript, 123 pp., 4to.

With corrections and a few additions in Beckett's hand.
Inscribed on the first page of text: "This is the original typescript / of my translation of the / American Anthology commissioned / by U.N.E.S.C.O. 1950 and / completed march or april of / that year. / First published December 1958 / by the Indiana University Press. / for Jake Schwartz / from his friend / Sam. Beckett / Paris february 1959."
Contains also two pages of notes, not in Beckett's hand, regarding the translation of specific words; together with a typed manuscript (some carbon copy) of "Antología de la Poesía Mexicana," with corrections and additions, mostly in another hand, 186 pp., 4to.

243. *Anthology of Mexican Poetry.* Translated by Samuel Beckett, compiled by Octavio Paz, preface by C. M. Bowra. Bloomington: Indiana University Press (1958). 8vo, original cloth, dust jacket.

With a presentation inscription on the half-title from Samuel Beckett to John [Kobler].
On the verso of the title page is the following translator's note:

> I should like to thank Mr. Gerald Brenan for kindly reading the entire manuscript and for making a number of useful suggestions.

S.B.

On 9 November 1961, Beckett wrote to Reavey, "The Mexican anthology was just an alimentary chore for UNESCO in 1950. I just got paid for the job and no further interest. No royalties. It should have been published by UNESCO but came out finally, much later, with Indiana University Press. Grove has no interest in this work. It is besides quite unimportant. The original poems, chosen by Paz, are execrable for the most part. My only excuse, which I know is not one, is that I was very broke at the time."

GEDICHTE
POEMS IN ENGLISH
POÈMES

The publication of Beckett's poems was a complex and intricately international affair. The first attempt at a collected edition was made in Wiesbaden by Limes Verlag, in 1959, under the title *Gedichte*. That edition included poems in French and in English, with German translations. On 21 February 1959, Beckett wrote to his friend George Reavey, "I am completely out of inédits in either language and am not succeeding in producing anything at the moment. No poems either. A trilingual edition of all the poems is to appear with the Limes Verlag (French & English originals and German translation). But they all [have] been published already somewhere or other."

When the news about *Gedichte* reached John Calder, Beckett's English publisher, he wrote to Limes Verlag on 29 April 1960, "We have decided to publish an English edition of the collected poems of Samuel Beckett.

"I understand that you have the world rights to many of the poems and that your edition has many of them in three languages. I wonder if you could send us a copy of your edition and at the same time let us know the position regarding rights, and a list of the poems where you control English rights."

Limes forwarded Calder's inquiry to Beckett, asking him to handle the matter with Calder, and on May 7th Beckett wrote to his editor in London, "Herewith your letter to Limes Verlag sent on by them to me with the request I should deal with the matter myself ('direkte Erledigung'), so no problem there. As soon as I can unearth the few other poems I have in English—some translated by me from the French, others unpublished—I shall send them along. I saw Barney Rosset the other day and he fully approves this edition of the poems."

Four days later, the Calder editor replied, asking for the titles of Beckett's poems which had been published in French only and not yet translated into English. On 7 July, Beckett answered:

> Herewith 4 poems translated from the French and one written in English (St-Lô) which does not figure in the Limes edition. The order I suppose should be:
> Whoroscope
> Echo's Bones
> Cascando (1936)
> St-Lô
> 4 translations.

On 24 July Beckett wrote, "I think it is preferable to exclude French poems from your edition and confine it to those written in English and the few—without original text—translated from the French. Apart from my preferring it that way there is the question of Minuit. I have always said to Jérôme Lindon that I did not want an edition of the French poems and he would not understand my letting them appear with you and not with him. Already he did not much relish their being published by Limes. . . . I hope you will not be too disappointed about this. There will be no further translations of French poems, so you can carry on with the texts you have. I shall need proofs needless to say."

Calder *was* disappointed, however, as his editor wrote to Beckett two weeks later: "He is tremendously keen to include the French poems. He stressed that he has absolutely no wish to do something with which you are not in agreement, but he is convinced that they should go into the book and is prepared to do anything you might suggest to persuade or placate M. Lindon. . . . I think he has some idea of printing them in small type at the back of the volume and hoping Minuit will not notice."

Three days later Beckett wrote back more firmly than before: "If you publish the French poems I shall have to consent to their publication by the Editions de Minuit. But I do not want them to appear in France at this stage. So I'm afraid I must insist again that they do not figure in your edition. I'm sorry."

In the fall of 1961, Reavey, who had brought the matter up in the first place, returned to the question: "I notice that Calder in London is announcing a book of poems. Which are these? I'd like to see a copy." Beckett replied (9 November 1961): "The Calder poems are composed of *Whoroscope, Echo's Bones* (with due acknowledgement to you & Europa) and odds and ends, some translated from the French. They should have been out long ago."

They finally did emerge from the press and on 10 December Beckett wrote the Calder editor:

> Thanks for your letter and six copies of *Poems*.
> I am very pleased with the book and wish I could say as much of the poems.

244. "Poèmes 38-39." In *Les Temps Modernes*, 2ᵉ année, No. 14 (November 1946). 8vo, original printed wrappers, uncut and unopened.

A few months earlier, Beckett had run into difficulties with Simone de Beauvoir over the publication of "Suite." (See No. 172.) But in spite of that "resounding difference of opinion," as he referred to it in a letter to Arland Ussher, this group of thirteen poems—all of them written before the war, in French—was printed in the November issue of *Les Temps Modernes*.

245. "They come . . ." [5-line poem]. In *Out of This Century. The Informal Memoirs of Peggy Guggenheim*. New York: The Dial Press, 1946. 8vo, original cloth with dust jacket, designed by Jackson Pollock.

First edition.
This is apparently the original printing of "a poem written by Oblomov" (the name given to Samuel Beckett by Peggy Guggenheim in her memoirs). It appeared in a French version as part of "Poèmes 38-39" in *Les Temps Modernes* (November 1946).

246. "Poème" ("que ferais-je sans ce monde sans visages sans questions"). Typed manuscript, 1 p., 4to.

   Typescript of the poem as it appeared in *Transition Forty-Eight*, No. 2 (1948). It varies slightly from the poem collected later in *Gedichte* and in subsequent editions of Beckett's poetry.
   From the collection of George Reavey.

247. "Trois Poèmes." In *Transition Forty-Eight*, No. 2. Editor Georges Duthuit. Paris: Transition Press, 1948. 12mo, original illustrated wrappers, uncut.

   The three poems, printed here for the first time, are "je suis ce cours de sable qui glisse," "que ferais-je sans ce monde sans visages sans questions," and "je voudrais que mon amour meure." They appear opposite Beckett's English translations ("my way is in the sand flowing," "what would I do without this world faceless incurious," "I would like my love to die").
   This issue contains also Beckett's unsigned translation of Henri Pichette's "Apoem 4" (Pichette's original French text is printed as well).

248. "Trois Poèmes." In *Les Cahiers des Saisons*, No. 2 (October 1955). 8vo, original wrappers, uncut.

   The three poems, printed here for the first time, are "Accul," "Mort de A.D.," and "vive morte ma seule saison."

249. *Gedichte.* Wiesbaden: Limes Verlag (1959). 12mo, original pictorial boards.

   First edition.
   Inscribed on the title page: "for Jake [Schwartz] / from Sam / friendship / Paris / Feb. 1960."
   This first collected edition contains all of Beckett's poems to date, in the original English or French, along with their German translations.

250. "Saint-Lô 1945." In *Rhinozeros*, 2. Episode (1960). 8vo, original pictorial wrappers.

   Idiosyncratic printing of this poem which first appeared in *Irish Times* and was later collected in *Poems in English* (see below).
   With a presentation inscription on the front cover to Jake [Schwartz].
   The back wrapper has a reproduction of a drawing by Jean Cocteau with his greeting to *Rhinozeros*.

251. *Poems in English.* London: John Calder (1961). Crown 8vo, original cloth, uncut.

Copy No. 2 of 100 copies on handmade paper, signed by the author, printed (*hors commerce*) "in advance of the first edition."
Inscribed on the title page: "for / Nancy [Cunard] / with love from / Sam / Paris July 1963."

252. *Poems in English.* London: John Calder (1961). 8vo, original blue cloth, dust jacket.

First edition, regular issue.
Inscribed on the title page: "for / Hugo Manning / with all good wishes / Samuel Beckett / Paris March 69."
With the L. W. Payne Collection bookplate.

253. *Poems in English.* New York: Grove Press (1963). 12mo, original cloth, dust jacket.

Inscribed on the title page: "Samuel Beckett."

254. *Poèmes.* [Paris] Les Editions de Minuit (1968). Square 12mo, original printed wrappers, uncut and unopened.

First edition. One of 100 numbered copies *hors commerce* on *vélin cuve B.F.K. Rives* of a total edition of 762.
Inscribed on the half-title: "for / John & Evelyn [Kobler] / with love / from Sam / Paris feb. 68."

255. "Kottabista." In *Hermathena: A Dublin University Review.* Offprint from No. CXV (Summer 1973). 8vo, original illustrated wrappers.

Beckett's rhymed version of one of Chamfort's *Maximes* ("Hope is a knave befools us evermore"), along with related correspondence, was his contribution to the centenary number of *Hermathena* and, in the words of the editor, "illustrate[s] his typically positive response to a request from his *alma mater.*"
With a presentation inscription signed "Sam Beckett."

256. "Long After Chamfort." In *The Blue Guitar* [Messina, 1975]. Offprint from Vol. I, No. 1. 8vo, original wrappers.

"Free rhymed adaptations of six *Maximes* by Sébastian [*sic*] Chamfort. All are unpublished except No. 6 which appeared in the Dublin University review *Hermathena*, CXV (Summer, 1973), [p.] 19."
In a letter to George Reavey on 9 August 1972, Beckett wrote: "Come here [Ussy] whenever I can get away, i.e. far too seldom for my liking. . . . Have disimproved some hours doggerelizing Chamfort's *Maximes*. Here is one may divert you:

Live & clean forget from day to day,
Mop life up as fast as it dribbles away."

With a presentation inscription, signed "Sam Beckett," on the title page.

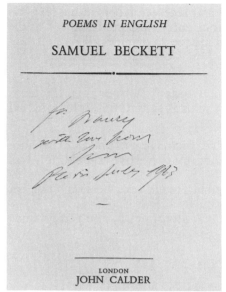

251   262

257. "Poèmes," In *Minuit*, No. 21 (November 1976). 8vo, original pictorial wrappers.

This issue of *Minuit* contains all the poems previously published in Les Editions de Minuit's 1968 collected edition, *Poèmes*, and includes, in addition, "hors crâne seul dedans," printed here for the first time. The date of this poem's composition seems to be uncertain: according to a note in *Poèmes suivi de mirlitonnades* (1978), where "hors crâne seul dedans" was later reprinted, the poem "was written in 1976," but in Calder's 1977 *Collected Poems in English and French*, it is printed under the title "Poème 1974."

258. *Collected Poems in English and French*. London: John Calder (1977). 12mo, original boards, dust jacket.

"This is the most complete collection of his poems that Mr. Beckett has authorised to date . . . all the work previously published in English with the addition of previously uncollected pre-war poems and some recent ones" [from the publisher's foreword].

259. *Poèmes [suivi de mirlitonnades, 1976-1978].* [Paris] Les Editions de Minuit (1978). Square 12mo, original printed wrappers, uncut and unopened. One of 106 numbered large-paper copies on *Alfamousse*.

260. "Act Without Words 2." Page proof from the first printing (see below), with autograph corrections and one revision in Beckett's hand, folio.

261. "Act Without Words 2." In *New Departures* 1 (Summer 1959). Crown 8vo, original wrappers.

First printing of this mime. Beckett wrote the work originally in French, but his English translation was published first.

115

Although Beckett had asked for and received proofs of his text, his corrections and addition (see previous entry) were not followed in the publication. (He had earlier refused to accept payment for his contribution.)

262. *Act Without Words 1. Act Without Words 2*. With original linoleum cuts by H. M. Erhardt [Stuttgart: Manus Presse, 1965]. Folio, original full sackcloth, in publisher's board case.

One of 10 numbered copies with an original pastel and an extra suite of the linoleum cuts signed in pencil by the artist. The edition was limited to 200 copies.
Trilingual edition, with the original French text, Beckett's English translation, and the German version by Elmar Tophoven.
". . . Erhardt was led to Beckett's Pantomimes by the performance given by Deryk Mendel. . . ."

Act Without Words II. See also Nos. 342, 352, 353.

263. "Acte sans paroles 2." In *Dramatische Dichtungen*, Band I. [Frankfurt am Main] Suhrkamp Verlag (1963). 8vo, original cloth, dust jacket.

First printing of Beckett's original French text, with facing German translation by Elmar Tophoven. This first volume contains also the first appearance in book form of *Cascando*, in its original French.
Other Beckett plays appearing in this two-volume, trilingual edition, either in the original French or English, with accompanying German translations, are: *Waiting for Godot, Endgame, Act Without Words I, All That Fall, Krapp's Last Tape, Play, Happy Days*, and *Words and Music*. The corresponding English or French versions of the plays appear at the end of each volume.

Acte sans paroles II. See also No. 308.

264. "The Goad. A Film Treatment by Paul Joyce of *Act Without Words II*." In *Nothing Doing in London* [No. 1]. London: Anthony Barnett (1966). Small folio, loose in sheets within original wrappers, as issued.

One of 500 numbered copies.
Inscribed by Beckett above the title of the film: "for John and Evelyn [Kobler], with love from Sam / Paris may 67."

265. "Embers." Carbon copy of typed manuscript, 10 pp., 4to.

With a few revisions and annotations in ink and in pencil, some of them in Beckett's hand.
The first page bears the autograph inscription, "Corrected Typescript of / *Embers* / for Jake Schwartz."
Embers, a radio play, was written for Jack MacGowran and Patrick Magee. It was produced by Donald McWhinnie for the BBC Third Programme, on 24 June 1959.

On 21 July, in a letter to Mary Manning Howe, Beckett wrote, "Heard a playback of Embers, good performance by Jack MacGowran and Kathleen Michael, but somehow it didn't come off I thought, my fault."

266. *Embers / Cendres.* Produced by Donald McWhinnie. BBC Third Programme, 24 June 1959. Duration: 45 minutes. Folio, original cloth-backed orange wrappers.

Beckett's radio play *Embers* was the winning BBC entry for the Italia Prize of 1959. The French version, *Cendres*, appears opposite the English text.

267. "Embers (A Play for Radio)." In *Evergreen Review*, Vol. III, No. 10 (November-December 1959). 12mo, original pictorial wrappers. First printing of this radio play.

Embers. See also Nos. 232, 233.

268. "Cendres." Typed manuscript, 14 pp., 4to.

With revisions and with other changes and annotations, some in Beckett's hand, in blue and red inks and in pencil.

An inscription at the head of page 1 reads: "Corrected typescript of / French translation of / 'Embers' ('Cendres') / for Jake Schwartz."

268

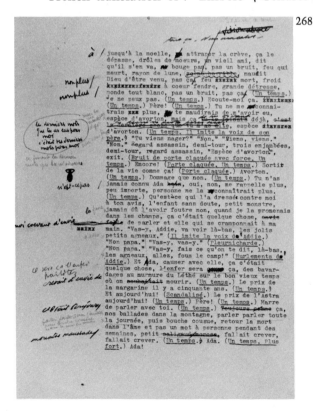

269. "Cendres (Embers). Pièce radiophonique." Translated from the English by Robert Pinget and the author. In *Les Lettres Nouvelles*, 7ᵉ année, Nouvelle Série, No. 36 (30 December 1959-January 1960). 8vo, original printed wrappers. First printing in French. Signed by Beckett on the first page of text.

Cendres. See also No. 236.

270. Robert Pinget. *La Manivelle.* Pièce Radiophonique. With facing English adaptation, *The Old Tune*, by Samuel Beckett. [Paris] Les Editions de Minuit (1960). 12mo, original printed wrappers, uncut.

First edition.
Inscribed on the half-title: "for Jake Schwartz / from / Sam Beckett / Paris March / 1961." Below the inscription, a printed label states in French that the English text of this radio play was broadcast for the first time in the BBC Third Programme on 21 August 1960, with Jack MacGowran as Cream and Patrick Magee as Gorman, directed by Barbara Bray.
In a letter to Reavey (20 November 1959) Beckett wrote, "This scribble . . . in haste to introduce to you my friend Robert Pinget, the most interesting young writer we have here in my opinion. Will you show him around a bit, I'd be very grateful."
On the verso of the final page of the Texas autograph manuscript of *En attendant Godot* and also on the last page of the fourth notebook ("Pim IV") of *Comment c'est*, Beckett has set up variant versions of title/cover arrangements for *La Manivelle*, which differ from each other and from the forms eventually followed.

271. Robert Pinget. "The Old Tune." English adaptation by Samuel Beckett. In *Evergreen Review*, Vol. V, No. 17 (March-April 1961). 8vo, original pictorial wrappers. First American printing.

272. Robert Pinget. *La Manivelle: The Old Tune.* English adaptation by Samuel Beckett. In *New Writers* II. London: John Calder (1962). 12mo, original boards, within dust jacket reproducing a photograph of Pinget and the other writers included. First English edition.

COMMENT C'EST
HOW IT IS

One of Samuel Beckett's most difficult works is the 'novel'—the single quotes are his—*Comment c'est*. He began work on it at his "shack" in the "spinachy Seine-et-Marne" near the end of 1958. Seven months later he wrote to Mary Manning Howe, "Struggling with another book in French, most difficult ever, nothing to do with theatre, another year to go if I can stick it." Five months later he wrote her, "I'm working hard (for me), but nothing to do with the theatre. Horribly difficult book and I don't see the end of it and can't do anything else." What had started as a compulsion had become an obsession.

By the end of the summer of 1960, Beckett stopped work on the book. Jérôme Lindon planned to bring it out at once. But the printer dragged his heels, in a curious throwback to other printers who, forty years earlier, had refused to set in type another distinguished Irish writer's work on the grounds that it was obscene; thus *Comment c'est* did not appear until the beginning of 1961. But even after publication, Beckett's troubles with the book were not over. On 9 November 1961 he wrote to Reavey, "Struggling to translate *Comment c'est*. Hopeless & depressing undertaking. Tempted to drop it." But drop it he didn't. He went on suffering through the translation and in the spring of 1964, *How It Is* appeared in New York and London.

273. "Comment c'est." Autograph manuscript, signed. Begun 17 December 1958 at Ussy, completed 6 January 1960 at Ussy, 477 pp., including 108 pp. of revisions completed at Ussy 7 June 1960, small 4to.

   This is the signed, original manuscript version of *Comment c'est*, first entitled "Pim," and written in blue, black, and red inks in six notebooks. Two of these contain sections of autograph revisions which Beckett has labeled "Révision I," "Révision II," and "Révision III." The cover of the first notebook has the autograph inscription, "Ce cahier et les 4 suivants numérotés de I à 5 constituent le manuscrit original de 'COMMENT C'EST'." The notebooks give evidence of the novel's having been written with hesitation and difficulty, as there are extensive revisions, deletions, and additions throughout. There are numerous doodles, some quite intricate in design, as well as complex calculations and diagrams.

274. "Comment c'est." Typed manuscript (some carbon copy), 88 pp., 4to.

   Enclosed in a red folder marked in Beckett's hand: "Comment c'est / (How It Is) / Typescript I." This typescript, like the two following, is divided into three parts. It has moderate to heavy autograph revisions,

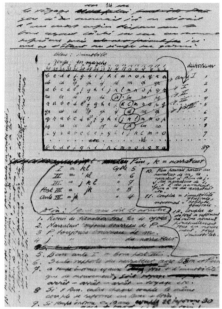 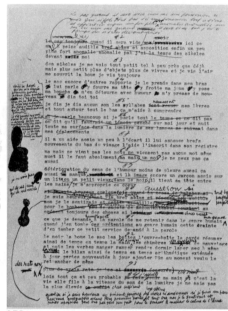

273   275

deletions, and additions in red and blue inks, some of them in Samuel Beckett's hand. In the margins, there are a few doodles and mathematical calculations and one diagram. Like the autograph manuscript, the typescript shows conventional punctuation and capitalization. In the third section Beckett has indicated, in red ink, the breaks where smaller paragraphs occur in subsequent typescripts.

The first page of Part II has the autograph note: "4 premières pages de cette partie données à la Revue 'Le 7' [*L'VII*], décembre 59." Beckett has deleted the title "Découverte de Pim." (These four pages are carbons.)

275. "Comment c'est." Typed manuscript (some carbon copy), 90 pp., 4to.

In a red folder; cover marked "Typescript II."

In this second typescript version, also made up of three parts, Beckett has discarded the traditional style of the earlier manuscripts (autograph manuscript and first typescript). The text has been extensively revised in red and blue inks and has numerous deletions and additions, as well as some organizational changes. Each paragraph is numbered. There are a few doodles and a number of mathematical calculations and diagrams.

Included with the typescript is a three-page carbon copy, with autograph corrections, of an extract entitled "L'Image," published in *X: A Quarterly Review* (November 1959).

276. "Comment c'est." Typed manuscript (some carbon copy), 88 pp., 4to.

In a red folder marked "Typescript III."

This typescript, which shows only a moderate amount of revision is close to the novel in its final form.

277. "L'Image." In *X: A Quarterly Review*, Vol. I, No. 1 (November 1959). Crown 8vo, original printed wrappers, uncut.

This excerpt from *Comment c'est* is an early and variant version taken from Part I and is the first appearance of the novel in any form. A corrected carbon of the typescript submitted to the review is included with the typed manuscript of *Comment c'est* (see above, "Typescript II") and represents an intermediate stage between the first and second typescripts.

Beckett has signed the first page of the extract underneath the title.

278. "Découverte de Pim." In *L'VII*, No. 1 (December 1959). Crown 8vo, original pictorial wrappers, uncut and unopened.

This is an extract from Part II of *Comment c'est*, derived from the first of the three typescript versions of the novel at the Humanities Research Center (see above, "Typescript I"). Beckett has signed the excerpt below the title, underneath his name.

279. *Comment c'est.* [Paris] Les Editions de Minuit (1961). 8vo, original wrappers, uncut and unopened.

First edition. One of 198 numbered copies on *Alfa Mousse Navarre*.
Inscribed on the title page: "for Jake [Schwartz] / from his friend / Sam. Beckett / Brighton March '61 / Original limited / edition."

280. *Comment c'est.* [Paris] Les Editions de Minuit (1961). 8vo, original wrappers, uncut and unopened.

First edition, regular issue.
Inscribed on the half-title: "for / Jake and Anita [Schwartz] / their friend / Sam / Paris jan. / 1961."

281. "From an Unabandoned Work." Extract from *How It Is* in *Evergreen Review*, Vol. IV, No. 14 (September-October 1960). 8vo, original pictorial wrappers.

Inscribed on the cover: "For Jake Schwartz / this extract from an untitled work / Sam Beckett."
This extract, from the opening pages of Beckett's English translation of *Comment c'est*, was published before the original French edition. It shows a substantial number of variants from the complete work as eventually published by Grove Press.

282. "How It Is." Extract from *How It Is (Comment c'est)*, translated from the French by the author. In *ARNA: The Journal of the Faculty of Arts, The University of Sydney* (July 1962). 8vo, original pictorial wrappers.

Beckett has signed the extract, which is a variant version of the opening of Part III. It is followed by a critical essay of his work entitled "No Symbols Where None Intended," by Niall Montgomery.

283. "From *How It Is.*" A new novel by Samuel Beckett, translated from the French by the author. In *The Paris Review*, Vol. VII, No. 28 (Summer-

Fall 1962). Paris Editor: Patrick Bowles. Crown 8vo, original pictorial wrappers.

This extract is a variant version of Part III.

284. "Conclusion of 'How It Is'." In *Transatlantic Review*, No. 13 (Summer 1963). Crown 8vo, original pictorial wrappers.

Beckett has signed the extract, which is taken from the ending of Part III.

285. *How It Is*. Translated from the French by the author. New York: Grove Press (1964). 8vo, original cloth, dust jacket. First American edition. Signed by Beckett on the title page.

286. *How It Is*. Translated from the French by the author. London: John Calder (1964). 8vo, original vellum, top edges gilt, uncut and unopened. One of a limited edition of 100 numbered copies on handmade paper, signed by Beckett.

287. V.S. Pritchett. "'How It Is.' By Samuel Beckett." Autograph manuscript, 4 pp., 4to.

A review of *How It Is*, published in the *New Statesman* (1 May 1964) under the title "No Quaqua."

> *How It Is* does point to one or two things in Beckett that have made him remarkable as a dramatist in the rich traditions of Irish farce. There is the peculiar unexpected affinity with Shaw. Both dramatists triumphed in the seemingly impossible: they made garrullousness [*sic*] dramatic, seriously and comically at the same time. Both make their comedies out of the conflict between their serious concerns—rational justice in Shaw, the injustice of having been born and waiting for release in Beckett—and the flooding in of meaninglessness which their obsessive wit and word power has made inevitable.

288. Photograph of Samuel Beckett, at age three, and his mother, taken by Dorothy Elvery, a neighbor in Foxrock.

This photograph undoubtedly evoked the passage of reminiscence that appears on page 19 of the original edition of *Comment c'est*, published in 1961 by Les Editions de Minuit. That passage appears on pages 16-17 of the author's translation (*How It Is*), as published by Calder & Boyars in 1964.

> . . . it's me all of me and my mother's
> face I see it from below it's like nothing I ever saw
>
> we are on a veranda smothered in verbena the scented sun
> dapples the red tiles yes I assure you

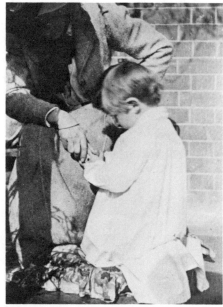

287   288

the huge head hatted with birds and flowers is bowed down
over my curls the eyes burn with severe love I offer her
mine pale upcast to the sky whence cometh our help and
which I know perhaps even then with time shall pass
away

in a word bolt upright on a cushion on my knees whelmed
in a nightshirt I pray according to her instructions

that's not all she closes her eyes and drones a snatch of the
so-called Apostles' Creed I steal a look at her lips

she stops her eyes burn down on me again I cast up mine in
haste and repeat awry

On Samuel Beckett's "Happy Days"

By George Reavey

for Sam

Three characters. A woman, a man, and an inscrutable universe.

How apposite the title Happy Days. How fitting for a play in our divided and impossible world of split memory, wavering illusion, and incredible reality. In our world of treaklish sentimentality and gross indifference. How expressive of the sentimental ostrich head-ensacked in a patch of potentially scorched earth -- the dry mound of our spilt tears, the unengraved grave of our mispent affections, the parch croak of our miscommunication.

In the breakdown of memory a few tenuous wisps of reminiscence struggling to affirm themselves, to implant their bare presence in the rootless air, like the dying gasps of a petering-out human motor clothed in the flesh of a once existent personal culture.

First. The great mother of us all -- young, old, and ageless -- still visible above the waist, but in the process of being sucked back into the pristine yellowing dust and grass, bequeathing as evidence of her existence nothing but a few paltry manmade objects, an almost empty bag (and black at that) of superfluous memorabilia -- a bottle of red/ medicine, a toothbrush, a magnifying glass. A tired parasol. And, excruciatingly, an incalculable revolver - the cast off property of Ibsen or Chekhov, tantalizing in its ineffectiveness, but no longer absolutely necessary except in the Congo.

HAPPY DAYS
OH LES BEAUX JOURS

Happy Days was first performed at the Cherry Lane Theatre in Greenwich Village on 17 September 1961. After attending a preview, George Reavey wrote to Beckett: "It sings in the memory, auricular and visual." He sent him his reactions—"white hot"—to which Beckett replied on 22 September, "I am very interested in your reactions. I did not write it with such things in mind—far too preoccupied with seeing and hearing it in its mere particularity. . . . I'm afraid for me it is no more than another dramatic object. I am aware vaguely of the hidden impetuses that are behind its making but their elucidation would prevent the making."

After his third visit to *Happy Days*, Reavey wrote again: ". . . a beautiful performance. Ruth White was really in her element and the lines came over with precision and feeling. The house was packed, and the applause high. . . . I laughed in a number of places as I had also done in *Fin de partie*, although some people here are too frightened to laugh. . . . They are all so depressed that they . . . say they don't want to be depressed any more and think your plays depressing, thus missing all the wit and humour."

The following February and again in June, Beckett wrote to Reavey about his plans to go to London for rehearsals of *Happy Days*, scheduled to open at the Royal Court on 11 October with Joan Plowright as Winnie. But by the time the play opened, on 1 November, the role of Winnie had been given to Brenda Bruce, Joan Plowright having become pregnant.

The French version—*Oh les beaux jours*—was previewed at the 22nd International Festival of Prose Drama in Venice on 28 September 1963 and opened in Paris at the Odéon—Théâtre de France on 15 November. Four months earlier, Beckett had written to Reavey: "Proofs, translations, rehearsals, so it goes. French *Happy Days* with Mad[eleine] Renaud & [Jean-Louis] Barrault opens at Odéon in October. There might be a bit of excitement in that—she is really keen."

289. *Happy Days. A Play in Two Acts.* New York: Grove Press (1961). 8vo, original decorative wrappers.

> First edition.
> Inscribed on the title page: "for John & Evelyn [Kobler] / affectionately / Sam / Ussy April / 69."

290. *Happy Days. A Play in Two Acts.* Mimeographed acting version. London: The English Stage Company, Royal Court Theatre [1962]. 4to, original cloth-backed rust covers. Signed by Beckett on the front cover.

291. *Happy Days. A Play in Two Acts.* London: Faber and Faber (1962). 8vo, original wrappers, uncut.

> Advance-proof copy of *Happy Days*, scheduled for publication on 15 June.
> Inscribed on the title page: "for / John & Evelyn [Kobler] / affectionately / Sam / Ussy april / 69."

292. *Happy Days. A Play in Two Acts.* London: Faber and Faber (1962). 8vo, original cloth, dust jacket illustrated with a photograph by Alix Jeffry of the original production of the play, with Ruth White and John C. Beecher, at the Cherry Lane Theatre, New York, 1961. First English edition, signed by Beckett on the title page.

293. "Happy Days." In *Seven Arts: Plays and Players*, Vol. X, No. 2 (November 1962). Folio, original pictorial wrappers.

294. *Happy Days.* Processed acting version. London: The National Theatre [1974?]. Folio, loose in sheets, within black paper covers.

Happy Days. See also No. 263.

295. *Oh les beaux jours.* [Paris] Les Editions de Minuit (1963). 8vo, original wrappers, uncut and unopened.

> First edition of the French translation. One of 87 numbered large-paper copies on *pur fil.*
> With a presentation inscription on the title page to John [Kobler].

Oh les beaux jours. See also No. 364.

296. George Reavey. "On Samuel Beckett's *Happy Days.*" Autograph manuscript, initialed, 16 September 1961, 3 pp., 4to; together with corrected typed manuscript of the same notes, with further autograph corrections and marked in red ink, *"for Sam,"* 3 pp., 4to.

> These are the "white-hot reactions" referred to in the opening paragraph of the *Happy Days* section of this catalogue. With a copy of the playbill.

297. Photograph showing Jessica Tandy as Winnie and Hume Cronyn as Willie in *Happy Days*, from the 1972 Samuel Beckett Festival in The Forum Theater at Lincoln Center. Together with a playbill.

298. "Words and Music." In *Evergreen Review*, Vol. VI, No. 27 (November-December 1962). 12mo, original pictorial wrappers.

> First printing of this radio play, broadcast by the BBC in their Third Programme on 13 November 1962, with Felix Felton and Patrick Magee as the two voices and with music by John Beckett. Produced by Michael Bakewell.

Words and Music. See also Nos. 263, 301, 305.

297

299. "Cascando. Invention radiophonique pour musique et voix." Musique de Marcel Mihalovici. Paroles de Samuel Beckett. In *L'VII*, Nos. 13 et 14 (3 April 1963). Crown 8vo, original decorative wrappers with cover design by Max Ernst.

First printing of *Cascando*, which Beckett wrote in French. Beckett's signature appears on the title page to his work.
This play for radio was first broadcast over the French national network program "France Culture" on 13 October 1963, with Roger Blin and Jean Martin.

300. "Cascando." Translated from the French by the author. In *Evergreen Review*, Vol. VII, No. 30 (May-June 1963). 12mo, original pictorial wrappers.

First printing in English of this radio play, broadcast in the BBC Third Programme on 6 October 1964 under the direction of Donald McWhinnie, with Patrick Magee as the Voice and Denys Hawthorne as the Opener. Music by Marcel Mihalovici.

301. *Cascando.* A radio play translated from the French by the author. Music by Marcel Mihalovici. In *Cascando and Other Short Dramatic Pieces.* New York: Grove Press (1968). 8vo, original decorative wrappers.

First American edition, published in both cloth and wrappers.
Inscribed on the title page: "for John [Kobler] from Sam / Paris feb. 1970."

In addition to *Cascando,* this collection includes *Words and Music, Eh Joe, Play, Come and Go,* and *Film.*

Cascando. See also Nos. 263, 305, 308.

Paroles et musique. See also Nos. 263, 308.

302. "Second Testament" ("Deuxième Testament"). In *Selected Poems* by Alain Bosquet. Translations by Samuel Beckett, Charles Guenther, Edouard Roditi, and Ruth Whitman. The World Poets Series [New York: New Directions, 1963].

This small collection of Alain Bosquet's poems contains selections—in the original French with accompanying English translations—from *Forgotten Kingdom* (1955), *First Testament* (1957), and *Second Testament* (1959). Beckett has translated three of the eighteen sections comprising the long poem "Ecrit en marge du poème," which appears as the last poem in *Deuxième Testament,* published by Gallimard. He has signed the translation below his printed name.

303. Alain Bosquet. *Deuxième Testament.* Paris: Gallimard (1959). 12mo, original printed wrappers, uncut and unopened.

Inscribed on the flyleaf: "Au poète / E. E. Cummings / en respectueux hommage, / Alain Bosquet." There is one textual emendation in Bosquet's hand in the back-cover text.

From the library of E. E. Cummings, and with his blind-stamp on the front cover.

PLAY
COMÉDIE

Play was written in English, translated into French, and then into German. But it was the German text, prepared by Elmar and Erika Tophoven with Beckett's assistance, that was first produced, as *Spiel*, in Ulm-Donau in June 1963, directed by Deryk Mendel, the actor-dancer who played in Beckett's mimes, *Act Without Words I* and *II*, on the same program. The American production, directed by Alan Schneider, opened at the Cherry Lane Theatre on 4 January 1964, and the London company, under the direction of George Devine, three months later at The Old Vic on 7 April.

To Jack MacGowran Beckett wrote of the French production on 23 September 1963:

> Start rehearsals with Madeleine [Renaud] next week. Afraid no chance of getting to London this "summer." Shall be over end of year or early next to assist George [Devine] in his production of *Play* for the National Theatre. [Jean-Marie] Serreau will do it here about the same time.

And to Reavey, on 13 April 1964:

> I have been going it pretty hard. I seem to have been rehearsing practically without pause since January. Just back from 3 weeks in London on rehearsals of *Play*. Very pleased with result—rather different from N.Y. from what I have heard. Start tomorrow—or rather resume—French verison [*Comédie*] with Serreau, opening next month. Then back to London in June for *Endgame* at the Aldwych. Then I hope a long retreat at Ussy to try and collect what wits remain.

Six weeks later, in a letter to MacGowran, he wrote, "Serreau rehearsals as impossible as ever. No stage yet. Lamp not working. And we are supposed to open tomorrow week! We are all crowned off & sick of the whole thing."

Comédie finally did open, although ten days late. Two years later, when it was revived, Beckett was, as before, deeply involved. He wrote to MacGowran on 8 September 1966, "Up to my eyes in theatre again for my sins and despite rows rerehearsing *Play* with new cast for new season at Théâtre de France. Hope to try it a different way. Serreau nominally in charge is off to Dallas (Texas)! and N.Y. for 10 days on theatre prospection, so no escape."

304. *Play*. Mimeographed acting version. New York: Theater 1964 / 38 Commerce Street. 4to, loose in sheets, within blue paper covers.

   Signed in ink on the front cover by Samuel Beckett. With variants from the published version in both text and stage directions.

305. *Play and Two Short Pieces for Radio.* London: Faber and Faber (1964). 12mo, original cloth, dust jacket.

> First edition.
> Inscribed on the title page: "for John [Kobler] from Sam / Paris April 66."
> The two radio plays are *Cascando* and *Words and Music.*

306. "Play." In *Evergreen*, Vol. VIII, No. 34 (December 1964). Folio, original wrappers.

> First American printing. The text is illustrated with a photograph by Alix Jeffry from the play's American premiere at the Cherry Lane Theatre.

> *Play.* See also Nos. 263, 301.

307. "Comédie. Un Acte de Samuel Beckett." Translated from the English by the author. In *Les Lettres Nouvelles*, 12ᵉ année, Nouvelle Série (June-July-August 1964). Square 12mo, original printed wrappers. First printing of Samuel Beckett's translation of his one-act drama, *Play.*

308. *Comédie. Pièce en un acte.* Translated from the English by the author. In *Comédie et actes divers.* [Paris] Les Editions de Minuit (1966). 8vo, original wrappers, uncut and unopened.

> First collected edition. One of 87 numbered copies on *pur fil Lafuma.*
> Inscribed on the title page: "for John [Kobler] / from Sam / Paris / April 66."
> This edition contains, in addition to *Comédie*, the "dramaticule" *Va et vient*, the radio plays *Cascando* and *Paroles et musique*, the television play *Dis Joe*, and the mime *Acte sans paroles II.*

309. "An Untitled Film Script ['Film']." In *Project I*. Three Original Motion Picture Scripts by Samuel Beckett, Eugène Ionesco, Harold Pinter. New York: Evergreen Theatre, [1964?]. Folio, loose in sheets within black binder.

> Mimeographed scenario of "Film," signed by Beckett on the title page. With a few manuscript corrections. Four xeroxed pages of "Further notes to Beckett film" laid in.
> Running twenty-two minutes, "Film" is Beckett's cinematic interpretation of Bishop Berkeley's *"Esse est percipi"*—to be is to be perceived: mind at the center of the universe. Directed by Alan Schneider and starring Buster Keaton, the film—silent, except for a "ssh" in the first part, and in black and white—explores "the inescapability of self-perception." Although philosophical in its outlook, the film's "climate," Beckett indicated in his script, was to be "comic and unreal. O [the 'object' half of Keaton—'sundered into object (O) and eye (E)'] should invite laughter throughout by his way of moving." "Film" never prospered commercially but it won a number

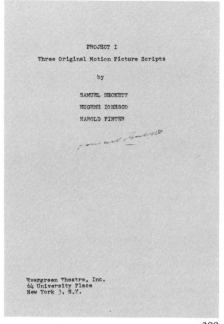 

309   312

of awards: in Venice, New York, and London film festivals (1965) and at Oberhausen, Tours, Sidney, and Krakow (1966).

310. *Film*. Complete scenario, illustrations, production shots. With an essay "On Directing 'Film'" by Alan Schneider. New York: Grove Press (1969). 12mo, original pictorial wrappers.

First separate printing of this text, not published in England until 1972.
Inscribed on the title page: "for John [Kobler] / from Sam / Paris / 1970."

Film. See also Nos. 301, 342.

311. *Film suivi de Souffle*. Translated from the English by the author. [Paris] Les Editions de Minuit (1972). Small 4to, original wrappers.

First appearance in book form of Beckett's translations of "Film" and *Breath*. One of 342 numbered copies on *vélin Arches*.
Inscribed on the title page: "for John and Evelyn [Kobler] / with love from Sam / Paris Nov. / 1972."

312 Photograph of Buster Keaton in "Film," 1964.

NEW YORK SHAKESPEARE FESTIVAL PRESENTS
A TRIBUTE
TO JACK MacGOWRAN
APRIL 30, 1973

June 27 1973   38 Bld. St.-Jacques
                 75014 Paris

Mr Andreas Brown
Gotham Book Mart
41 West 47th St.
New York City

Dear Mr Brown,

All I can find to offer is the unfinished
text herewith. It was written 1964 on the
rocky road to _Imagination morte imaginez_ and
then laid aside. It has never appeared anywhere in whole or in part. Apart from a few
cuts and corrections of detail I have made
no effort to improve it. The title remains to
be found. All proceeds from your edition and from
eventual foreign editions and subsidiary rights
would go to the MacGowran fund.

Needless to say the consent of Grove Press
(and of Calder & Boyars if the book were for
sale in U.K.) is an indispensable prerequisite.
No doubt an arrangement could be made whereby,
after a period to be agreed on, the rights
would revert to my habitual publishers. I have
explained the position and sent a copy of the
text to Mr Barney Rosset.

        With all good wishes, I am
        Yours sincerely

        Samuel Beckett

See page 133 and entry no. 317

132

FAUX DÉPARTS
ALL STRANGE AWAY
IMAGINATION MORTE IMAGINEZ
IMAGINATION DEAD IMAGINE

LE DÉPEUPLEUR
THE LOST ONES
BING
PING

In the mid-1960s, when Beckett was intensely involved with the theater, his prose (which he has always considered "the important writing") began to acquire its spare, but crystalline, characteristics. The route to these flawless gems was at all times a difficult and exacting one, resulting, often, in abandoned texts that differed from the works which eventually evolved from them, yet bore a strong family resemblance to them. Often the jettisoned works were picked up farther down the road and published separately, under their own titles.

The composition of *All Strange Away*, for example—which wasn't published until 1976, and then as a special project occasioned by Jack MacGowran's death—preceded that of *Imagination morte imaginez* and, in fact, gave birth to it. *Imagination morte imaginez* is a smaller version of *All Strange Away*, but it has been re-created to the point of being an independent work. It was published in 1965 and was immediately followed, in the same year, by its English translation. Three French fragments labeled "Faux Départs," all related to the published version of *Imagination morte imaginez* and linked with a fourth fragment, in English, which is clearly an earlier form of *All Strange Away*, appeared in *Kursbuch* I. These fragments hint at the possibility of the existence of a longer manuscript in French akin to *All Strange Away*, but no such manuscript has yet turned up.

The relationship of *Bing* to *Le Dépeupleur* is a similar one. Beckett began *Le Dépeupleur* in October 1965 and worked on it through May 1966. He then laid it aside, because of its unwieldiness, to start anew. The work which sprang from Beckett's struggle with *Le Dépeupleur* was *Bing*. It was finished five months after he had abandoned the first text and was published in the year of its completion, 1966. Markedly dissimilar to *Le Dépeupleur* in length, style, tone, and content, *Bing* is nevertheless a derivative of the earlier work—thematically, in particular: a reconstitution *in parvo* of two extracts from *Le Dépeupleur* which appeared prior to its publication in 1970, "Dans le cylindre" and "L'Issue."

Most of the short pieces Beckett has written in recent years are a condensation and a refinement of themes he had explored earlier at greater length. The stripping away of inherited "Anglo-Irish exuberance and automatisms" which marked his official passage from English to French has never ceased and is as evident today in his original and translated English texts as ever it was in French.

The same process continues in his theater—the "theatrical chamber music" in which everything counts: every syllable, every sigh, every pause.

"I don't expect I'll have any more big ones," Beckett told a friend in the summer of 1981. And the works do continue to grow shorter. But not necessarily slighter. Like Rembrandt's smaller drawings, these are monumental miniatures.

The direction is clear; the means, also, as a study of the unpublished manuscripts at the end of this catalogue will confirm. The destination, if not *as* clear, will surely become so—or more nearly so—in the years ahead.

313. "Faux Départs." In *Kursbuch* I (June 1965). 8vo, original printed wrappers.

> This work is divided into four sections, three in French and one in English. The French sections resemble passages in *Imagination morte imaginez* but vary in a way that suggests these segments are an earlier version of the published text. The single English section—more an adaptation than a strict translation of the preceding passages in French—corresponds to the opening lines of *All Strange Away*, a text written en route to *Imagination morte imaginez* and temporarily set aside. The passage printed here, in *Kursbuch*, contains substantive variants from the full text of *All Strange Away* published in 1976. Elmar Tophoven's translation of all four sections into German follows.
> Beckett has signed the text, next to the title.

314. *Imagination morte imaginez.* [Paris] Les Editions de Minuit (1965). 12mo, original printed wrappers, uncut and unopened.

> First edition. One of 612 numbered copies on *vélin cuve B.F.K. Rives.*
> Inscribed on the half-title: "for John [Kobler] / from Sam / Paris April / 66."

315. *Imagination Dead Imagine.* Translated from the French by the author. London: Calder and Boyars (1965). 12mo, original gilt-decorated buckram.

> First edition in English. Copy No. 2 of 100 copies on handmade paper, signed by the author and printed (*hors commerce*) in advance of the first edition.
> Inscribed on the title page: "for / John & Evelyn [Kobler] / with love from Sam / Paris / march 67."

316. "Imagination Dead Imagine." In *Evergreen*, Vol. X, No. 39 (February

1966]. 4to, original illustrated wrappers. First American printing.

Imagination Dead Imagine. See also Nos. 193, 363.

317. "All Strange Away." Photocopy of corrected typescript (corrections in Beckett's hand), 1976, 10 pp., including a maquette of the colophon, folio.

With notes for the printer in another hand, in red, blue, and orange inks and in pencil. Contains variants from the published version.

When Jack MacGowran died at the end of January 1973, a benefit committee was set up to raise funds for his widow and daughter. As a member of that committee, Andreas Brown of the Gotham Book Mart asked Samuel Beckett to contribute "some short piece of writing" which could be published to provide additional income for the family. Beckett sent him on 27 June an "unfinished text . . . written 1964 on the rocky road to *Imagination morte imaginez* and then laid aside. Apart from a few cuts and corrections I have made no effort to improve it. The title remains to be found. All proceeds from your edition and from eventual foreign editions and subsidiary rights," he specified, "would go to the MacGowran fund." The title became *All Strange Away*, and the book, with illustrations by Edward Gorey—"a beautiful edition," Beckett wrote—reached him in Paris on 12 April 1977.

The first three words of this typescript—"Imagination dead imagine"—form the title of the work which eventually emerged from this early draft. In fact, *Imagination Dead Imagine* can be seen as a reduction of *All Strange Away:* (a) both take place inside a tomblike enclosure, with rotunda; (b) both deal with dead bodies, but living imaginations, which, in the course of the narratives, turn upon imagining death. The point of view of *Imagination Dead Imagine* is objective, but that of *All Strange Away* is more precise, with complex and characteristically Beckettian minute details: for example, a long, explicitly detailed account of a woman named Emma in *All Strange Away* is reduced to "the long hair of strangely imperfect whiteness, the white body of a woman finally" in *Imagination Dead Imagine;* and (c) silence, whiteness, light, and heat are significant elements in both texts. In short, the two works are thematically the same, but differ widely in length, descriptive approach, and perspective.

318. "All Strange Away." Galley proofs, as revised by Samuel Beckett, with additional notes, in other hands, to the printer, 8 March 1976, 6 pp., folio.

319. "All Strange Away." Unbound sheets [1976], 19 pp., small folio.

Written on the flyleaf: "Unique first / state of sheets / (with 'error')"; and on page 16: "This error was discovered before / sheets left printer. New gathering / reprinted—then sent to binder. / A. B. [Andreas Brown]."

320. *All Strange Away.* With illustrations by Edward Gorey. [New York]

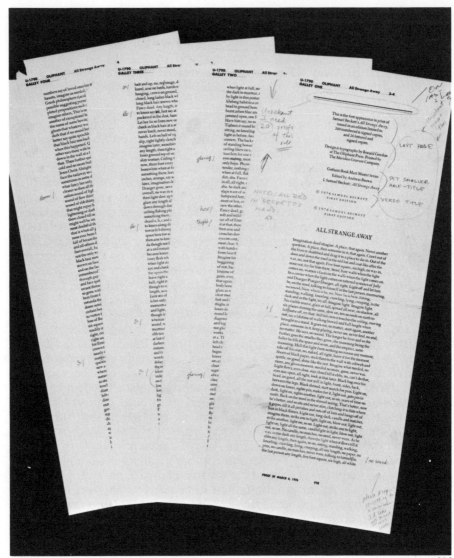

318

Gotham Book Mart (1976). Small folio, original morocco-backed decorative boards, in publisher's slipcase.

One of 200 numbered copies signed by the author and the artist. Inscribed on the colophon: "for / University of Texas Collection / Samuel Beckett."

321. "All Strange Away." In *Journal of Beckett Studies*, No. 3 (Summer 1978). 8vo, original wrappers, illustrated with a photograph by Heinz Köster of the 1975 German production of *Waiting for Godot* at the Schiller-Theater. First English printing.

All Strange Away. See also No. 409.

Vu du sol le mur sur tout son pourtour et sur toute sa
hauteur présente une surface ininterrompue. Et cependant
sa moitié supérieure est criblée de niches. Ce paradoxe
s'explique par la nature de l'éclairage dont l'omni-
présence escamote les creux. Sans parler de sa faiblesse.
Chercher d'en bas une niche des yeux ne s'est jamais vu.
Il est rare que les yeux se lèvent. Quand ils le font c'est
vers le plafond. Sol et mur sont vierges de toute marque
pouvant servir de point de repère. Des échelles dressées
toujours aux mêmes endroits les pieds ne laissent pas de
traces. Les coups de tête et de poing contre le mur non
plus. Il y aurait des marques que l'éclairage empêcherait
de les voir. Le grimpeur qui emporte son échelle pour la
dresser à un autre endroit le fait un peu au jugé. Il est
rare qu'il se trompe de plus de quelques centimètres. Du
fait de la disposition des niches l'erreur maximale n'est
que d'un mètre environ. Sous l'effet de sa passion son
agilité est telle que même cet écart ne l'empêche pas de
gagner une niche quelconque sinon celle de son choix
ni à partir d'elle quoique plus difficilement de regagner
l'échelle d'un vaincu ou mieux d'une vaincue ou mieux
encore de la vaincue. Elle est assise contre le mur les
jambes relevées. Elle a la tête entre les genoux et les
bras autour des jambes. La main gauche tient le tibia
droit et la droite l'avant-bras gauche. Les cheveux roux
ternis par l'éclairage arrivent jusqu'au sol. Ils lui cachent
le visage et tout le devant du corps jusqu'à l'entrejambes.
Le pied gauche est croisé sur le droit. Elle est le nord. Elle
plutôt que les autres vaincus à cause de sa fixité plus
grande. A qui exceptionnellement veut faire le point elle
peut servir. Telle niche pour le grimpeur peu enclin aux
acrobaties évitables peut se trouver à tant de pas ou de
mètres à l'est ou à l'ouest de la vaincue sans naturellement
qu'il la nomme ainsi ou autrement même en pensée. Il va
de soi que seuls les vaincus se cachent le visage. Ils ne le

(inédit)
par SAMUEL BECKETT

dans
le
cylindre

325

328

SAMUEL BECKETT

SÉJOUR

JEAN DEYROLLE

G. R. PARIS 1970

137

322. *Bing.* [Paris] Les Editions de Minuit (1966). 12mo, original printed wrappers, uncut and unopened.

First edition. One of 100 numbered copies *hors commerce* of an edition of 762 on *vélin cuve B.F.K. Rives.*
Inscribed on the half-title: "for / John & Evelyn [Kobler] / affectionately / Sam / Paris Nov. / 66."

323. *Bing.* Text in German, translated by Elmar Tophoven. With embossed illustrations by H. M. Erhardt. [Stuttgart] Manus Presse, 1970. Folio, loose in sheets within black-cloth folding case. Edition limited to 60 numbered copies. The plates, printed on *papier Arches,* are numbered and signed in pencil by the artist.

324. "Ping." In *Encounter,* Vol. 28, No. 2 (February 1967). Small 4to, original printed wrappers.

First printing in English.
A segment of *Bing,* translated by the author. (See also Nos. 193, 363.)

325. "Dans le cylindre." In *Livres de France: Revue littéraire mensuelle,* XVIIIe année, No. 1 (January 1967). Small folio, original wrappers illustrated with a photographic portrait of Samuel Beckett by Guy Suignard.

Special issue devoted principally to Beckett. Inscribed "for John & Evelyn [Kobler] / with love from Sam." Beckett has added two lines to the text and made one additional correction in ink.
This then-unpublished passage from a text written in 1966 appeared in its complete form in 1970 as *Le Dépeupleur* (see No. 329). It is the same passage which appears in *The North,* published in 1972 and illustrated by Avigdor Arikha (No. 331).

326. "La Notion." In *L'Ephémère,* No. 13 (Spring 1970). Small 4to, original pictorial wrappers.

A prepublication extract, with minor variants, from *Le Dépeupleur* (second paragraph).
Inscribed by the author, beneath his printed name: "for John & Evelyn [Kobler] / with love from Sam / Paris june 1971."

327. *L'Issue.* With six original engravings by Arikha. Paris: Les Editions Georges Visat [1968]. 4to, loose in sheets within original embossed wrappers, uncut, and publisher's slipcase.

The edition was limited to 154 numbered copies on *grand vélin de Rives,* printed in 28-point Caslon Old Style by Fequet et Baudier. Each of Arikha's engravings is signed in pencil by the artist.
With autograph inscriptions on the half-title from the author and the artist to "John and Evelyn [Kobler]."
This is the first printing of this text, which is a passage (third and fourth paragraphs) from *Le Dépeupleur* containing substantive variants from the first complete published edition.

328. *Séjour*. With engravings by Louis Maccard from the original drawings by Jean Deyrolle. Paris: G. R. [Georges Richar] 1970. Oblong 8vo, loose in sheets within original wrappers, uncut, in publisher's folding box.

One of 150 numbered copies on *grand vélin de Rives à la forme* of a total edition of 175. Signed in ink by Samuel Beckett and stamped with the facsimile signature of Jean Deyrolle, to whom Beckett had given the text to illustrate but who had died before completing the project. (The text consists of the first paragraph, with minor variants, of the then-unpublished *Le Dépeupleur*.) Beckett selected from a group of thirty-two preparatory drawings the five which were engraved for this edition.
    The text was printed in 20-point Caslon Old Face by Fequet et Baudier; the engravings, on the hand-press of Georges Leblanc.
    Inscribed: "for John & Evelyn [Kobler] / with love from Sam / Paris September / 1970."
    The original prospectus is laid in.

329. *Le Dépeupleur*. [Paris] Les Editions de Minuit (1970). 12mo, original printed wrappers, uncut and unopened.

First edition. One of 106 numbered copies on *pur fil Lafuma*.
    Inscribed on the half-title: "for John & Evelyn [Kobler] / with love from Sam / Paris Jan. 1971."
    The original prospectus is laid in.

330. "The Lost Ones." Extract printed in *The New York Times*, one full page, 16 December 1972.

On 19 December, Reavey wrote to Beckett: "The sensation of the season, I think, came on Saturday Dec. 16th, namely the printing by NY Times of a whole page of your *Lost Ones*. I enclose it. It shld surprise you too."

331. *The North*. With three original etchings by Avigdor Arikha. London: Enitharmon Press, 1972. Folio, loose in sheets, within original embossed wrappers, uncut, and publisher's linen slipcase.

The edition, limited to 137 numbered copies, was printed by Will and Sebastian Carter at the Rampant Lions Press, Cambridge, hand-set in Palatino on paper made by J. Barcham Green, Maidstone. The text is the next-to-the-last paragraph in *The Lost Ones* and contains minor variants from the full edition in English.
    This copy is signed "Sam. Beckett" and bears, below the signature, a presentation inscription in Beckett's hand: "for / John & Evelyn [Kobler] / with love from Sam / Paris Nov. 1972." Each of Arikha's original etchings is signed in pencil by the artist.

332. *The Lost Ones*. Translated from the original French by the author. London: Calder and Boyars (1972). 8vo, original half-leather, all edges gilt, in publisher's slipcase. First English edition. One of 100 copies "signed by the author and specially bound . . . printed in advance of the first edition."

333. *The Lost Ones.* Translated from the original French by the author. New York: Grove Press (1972). 8vo, original printed wrappers. First American edition.

334. "The Lost Ones." Illustrated by Philippe Weisbecker. In *Evergreen*, Vol. XVII, No. 96 (Spring 1973). 12mo, original illustrated wrappers.

335. Two cables exchanged by Jean Reavey and Samuel Beckett concerning a "reading" of *The Lost Ones.* New York and Berlin, 10 and 12 February 1975.

Through Jean Reavey, the acting company Mabou Mines requested permission for a reading of *The Lost Ones* to accompany their production of *Play* and *Come and Go.* Beckett cabled his approval for a "straight reading." The result proved to be a highly original dramatic presentation featuring David Warrilow and a female member of the Company, both in the nude. On 10 April 1975, Beckett wrote to Jean Reavey: "Sounds a crooked straight reading to me."

336. "Assez." Un texte inédit de Samuel Beckett. In *La Quinzaine Littéraire*, No. 1 (15 March 1966). Folio, original wrappers.

Although "Assez" is here labeled "unpublished," printing of the first edition (see below) was completed on 19 February, and the edition was presumably available in the bookshops shortly thereafter.

337. *Assez.* [Paris] Les Editions de Minuit (1966). Square 12mo, original printed wrappers, uncut and unopened.

First edition. One of 762 numbered copies printed on *vélin cuve B.F.K. Rives.*
Inscribed on the half-title: "for John [Kobler] from Sam / Paris april 1966."

Enough. See Nos. 193, 363.

338. "Samuel Beckett," by David Levine. Pen-and-ink, 16 x 11 cm., signed lower right, "D. Levine 67."

338a. Photographic portrait of Samuel Beckett by Guy Suignard, ca. 1966.

EH JOE
DIS JOE

Eh Joe, like *Embers* before it, was written for the actor Jack MacGowran, whom Beckett had met when the BBC Third Programme broadcast *All That Fall* in 1957. Over the years Beckett had become very fond of MacGowran, both man and actor. He worked closely with him in the preparation of "End of Day," MacGowran's one-man show consisting of readings from Beckett's work, which he assembled for a Dublin opening in October 1962, and then took to London. That idea later developed into another one-man performance which MacGowran called "Beginning to End," with which he had a measure of success in the United States. With Beckett's help, "Beginning to End" reached the Berlin Festival at the Schiller-Theater in 1971, where it was a hit.

Flexing himself in the direction of what was to become *Eh Joe*, Beckett wrote to MacGowran on 4 July 1963: "I haven't a gleam for the new work for you at the moment and feel sometimes that I've come to the end. It's a comfort to know you understand and won't press me." But by 15 May 1965, things were very different:

> Herewith script revised. . . . I'm sending copies to Donald [McWhinnie] and Margaret McLaren, who handles TV contracts for Curtis Brown.
>
> I hope I did not seem to assume that you would necessarily want to do it because it comes from me. I assure you I don't. I do hope you will take it on. But if on reading it again and thinking it over you decide it is not for you, no one will better understand than I.

Later that summer, after surgery on his jaw, Beckett wrote (30 August 1965):

> The op[eration] last month did not come off and will have to be done again. Not serious, no great urgency. But it would be a help if I could have approx[imate] dates for *Eh Joe* (your and Donald's trip to Paris & production date) as soon as possible, so that I can arrange op[eration] at a time I'm not needed. I would of course like the world first to be London and you, but I won't be able to hold up other productions indefinitely. Stuttgart notably have laid it on for next April & I have promised to give them a hand. I have finished the French translation and shall offer it to Madeleine [Renaud] & Jean-Louis [Barrault]. . . .
>
> John [Calder] thought Billie Whitelaw a possibility for *Eh Joe*. That would be fine with me, if for you.

As it turned out, neither McWhinnie nor Whitelaw was involved when *Eh Joe* was televised by the BBC on 4 July 1966.

141

339. "Eh Joe. A Piece for Television." Typed manuscript, 4 pp. plus title page, 4to.

Title page marked in red ink, in Beckett's hand, "TS 3 / I." With some autograph corrections and revisions.

340. "Eh Joe. A Piece for Television." Photocopy of typed manuscript, 4 pp., plus title page, 4to.

With autograph notations (directions for performance) in an unidentified hand, presumably Jack MacGowran's, as this script appears, on the basis of internal evidence (and provenance), to be MacGowran's rehearsal copy. The title page bears the label, "Curtis Brown, Ltd., 13 King Street, Covent Garden, / W.C. 2" and the manuscript note "Giacometti tree from Serreau." (The sculptor Alberto Giacometti had "made" a tree for the 1961 *Godot* revival at the Odéon. It has since disappeared.)

The verso of each of the five sheets has, in the same hand, notes about and quotations from some of Beckett's works. On the verso of the title page are notes apparently made for the recording of an LP album based on "End of Day" and arranged by Claddagh Records, an Irish firm founded by Gareth Brown.

341. *Eh Joe and Other Writings*. London: Faber and Faber (1967). 12mo, original printed wrappers.

Uncorrected proof copy, with a presentation inscription to John Kobler on the half-title.

342. *Eh Joe and Other Writings*. London: Faber and Faber (1967). 12mo, original cloth, dust jacket illustrated with a photograph of Jack MacGowran in the BBC 2 television production of *Eh Joe*, July 1966.

First collected edition, including *Act Without Words II* and *Film*. Inscribed on the title page: "for John & Evelyn [Kobler] / with love from Sam / Paris May 67."

343. "Eh Joe. A Television Play." In *Evergreen*, Vol. XIII, No. 62 (January 1969). 4to, original pictorial wrappers.

First American printing.

The text is illustrated with stills from the WNDT-TV production of the play, with George Rose as Joe and Rosemary Harris as the voice of the Woman.

Eh Joe. See also No. 301.

Dis Joe. See No. 308.

344. "Beginning to End. An Anthology of the Works of Samuel Beckett Adapted by Jack MacGowran." Photocopy of typed production script. New York, Shakespeare Festival [1970?], 49 pp., 4to.

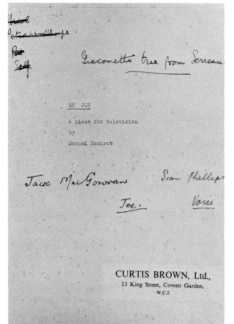

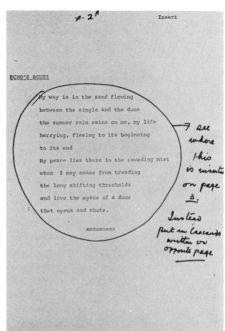

340   344

With autograph additions, deletions, and revisions.

Inscribed on the title page: "For John [Kobler] — / with affection and admiration / Jack MacGowran / September 1971." A note in MacGowran's hand above the title reads: "Revised / and / up-to-date."

This revised version of "Beginning to End" is composed of passages from *Malone Dies, Embers, Echo's Bones, Molloy, Cascando, Waiting for Godot, Watt, Words and Music, Krapp's Last Tape, Endgame*, and *The Unnamable*.

345. *Come and Go. Dramaticule.* London: Calder and Boyars (1967). Illustrated with photographs by Ilse Buhs of Deryk Mendel's Berlin production at the Schiller-Theater. 12mo, original gilt-decorated buckram, in publisher's slipcase.

First edition in English. One of a limited edition of 100 numbered copies on heavy coated stock, specially bound and signed by the author.

346. "Come and Go. Dramaticule." In the brochure, *The Arts and Censorship.* [London] The National Council for Civil Liberties and The Defense of Literature and the Arts Society [1968]. Folio, original pictorial wrappers.

Samuel Beckett's short play *Come and Go* was presented as part of "a gala entertainment concerning depravity and corruption" sponsored by the N.C.C.L. and the D.L.A.S. It was directed by Deryk Mendel, with Adrienne Corri, Marie Kean, and Billie Whitelaw in the roles of Flo, Vi, and Ru.

143

Depravity and Corruption

346   347

The brochure contains, as well, a poem by Alexander Trocchi, "lessons for boys & girls," which Trocchi has signed and dated in ink.

Come and Go. See also Nos. 301, 352, 353.

Va et vient. See No. 308.

347. Samuel Beckett in 1968. Photograph by the Swedish photographer Lüfti Özkök. Inscribed, lower left, "Pour Sam / L. Ö. 1968."

348. "Breath." Autograph manuscript, signed, 1969, 1 p., 4to.

With one autograph deletion. Signed by Beckett and dated, "Paris May 69."

349. ["Breath"]. Appearing as "Prologue" in *Oh! Calcutta! An Entertainment with Music.* Mimeographed acting script. New York: Elkins Productions International Corporation [1969?]. Folio, black binder.

Beckett's first stage direction, in the manuscript he submitted to Kenneth Tynan, reads: "Faint light on stage littered with miscellaneous rubbish." In the acting script and the Grove Press edition (see below), the period was replaced by a comma followed by "including naked people." As a result of that unauthorized addition and other ambiguities, Beckett refused to allow *Breath* to be included in the London production of *Oh! Calcutta!*

350. ["Breath"]. Appearing as "Prologue" in *Oh! Calcutta! An Entertainment with Music.* Devised by Kenneth Tynan. Directed by Jacques

144

Levy. New York: Grove Press (1969). 8vo, original cloth, dust jacket. First printing.

351. "Breath." With an introduction by John Calder and a reproduction of Beckett's autograph manuscript. In *Gambit: International Theatre Review*, Vol. IV, No. 16 [1970?]. 8vo, original pictorial wrappers. The cover includes a photograph of Samuel Beckett at a rehearsal for the Royal Court Theatre's production of the unexpurgated *Waiting for Godot*.

First English appearance.
John Calder's introduction traces the history of Beckett's involvement in *Oh! Calcutta!*: "The extreme brevity of this play without characters [*Breath*] is another step in the continual economy that has characterized Mr. Beckett's work in recent years. . . . Here in thirty seconds the complete statement [of man's tragedy] is made."

352. *Breath and Other Shorts*. London: Faber and Faber (1971). 8vo, original printed wrappers.

Uncorrected proof copy, inscribed on the title page: "for / John & Evelyn [Kobler] / with love from Sam / Paris April 1972."
The collection includes *Come and Go, Act Without Words I, Act Without Words II, From an Abandoned Work*, and *Breath*.

348

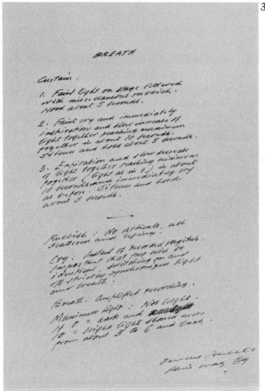

353. *Breath and Other Shorts.* London: Faber and Faber (1971). 8vo, original cloth, dust jacket. First English edition. With a presentation inscription to John and Evelyn [Kobler] on the title page.

Breath. See also No. 363.

354. "Souffle. Intermède." In *Les Cahiers du Chemin* 12 [Paris: La Nouvelle Revue Française, 15 April 1971]. 12mo, original printed wrappers.

> First printing of Beckett's translation of *Breath.*
> Inscribed above the title and Beckett's name: "for John & Evelyn [Kobler] / with love from Sam / Paris juin 1971."

Souffle. See also No. 311.

355. *Sans.* [Paris] Les Editions de Minuit (1969). Square 12mo, original printed wrappers, uncut and unopened.

> First edition. One of 742 numbered copies on *vélin cuve B.F.K. Rives.*
> Inscribed on the title page: "for John [Kobler] from Sam / Paris feb. 1970."

356. "Lessness." In *Evergreen*, Vol. XIV, No. 80 (July 1970). Small 4to, original illustrated wrappers.

> First American publication of Beckett's English translation of *Sans.*

357. *Lessness.* London: Calder & Boyars (1970). 12mo, original half-leather, all edges gilt, in publisher's slipcase. First English edition. One of 100 copies, "signed by the author and specially bound . . . printed (*hors commerce*) in advance of the first edition."

358. *Lessness.* Mimeographed radio script, 1971, 11 pp., folio.

> The script for a reading of Beckett's short prose text for BBC radio transmission on 25 February 1971. The cast included Donal Donnelly, Leonard Fenton, Denys Hawthorne, Patrick Magee, Harold Pinter, and Nicol Williamson. Produced by Martin Esslin.
> With two variants from the published version.

THE NOBEL PRIZE

In 1969, Beckett was awarded the Nobel Prize in Literature "for his writing in new forms for the novel and drama in which the destitution of modern man acquires its elevation." Five years earlier Sartre had turned down the prize. Beckett, a courteous and gentle man, would have found that response ungracious, no doubt. However, in keeping with his distaste for publicity and ceremonial occasions, he didn't go to Stockholm to receive his prize but was represented by his publisher, Jérôme Lindon.

Alfred Nobel had stipulated in his will that the prize should go to "uplifting" literary works. The Secretary of the Swedish Academy explained its choice this way: "The degradation of humanity is a recurrent theme in Beckett's writing, and to this extent his philosophy, simply accentuated by elements of the grotesque and of tragic farce, can be said to be a negativism that knows no haven." But, he continued, "the perception of human degradation is not possible if human values are denied. This is the source of inner cleansing, the life force in spite of everything, in Beckett's pessimism." And he concluded, "the writing of Samuel Beckett rises like a *miserere* from all mankind, its muffled minor key sounding liberation to the oppressed and comfort to those in need."

Since the publishing business is never slow to rise to such occasions, Beckett was pressured from both sides of the Atlantic to feed something quickly into its voracious maw. Finally, and almost *à contrecoeur*, he turned over to Les Editions de Minuit a story—"Premier Amour"—which he had written in 1946 but had withheld from publication. It came out in 1970, and Beckett worked slowly and with little satisfaction at an English translation—"First Love"—which was not published in England until 1973 and in America, until 1974.

359. "Premier Amour." Autograph manuscript, signed. Begun October 28 [1946], completed 12 November 1946, 58 pp., in small-4to bound exercise book.

   Written in ink, with frequent deletions, some additions, and revisions in ink and in pencil. One chart; doodles throughout. The cover is signed and marked "1945–1946 / unpublished / jettisoned."
   The "notes" with which the two final pages are "filled" (Admussen, p. 81) are Beckett's translations into French of two tributes to his friend Alfred Péron, who had died at the end of the war as a result of his treatment in a German concentration camp. These articles had appeared in the *Irish Times*, one of them by Alex Vickmann, a friend of Péron's from his Trinity College days.

360. "Premier Amour." Photocopy of typed manuscript showing Beckett's revisions, but in another hand, 1964, 32 pp., 4to, in a looseleaf binder.

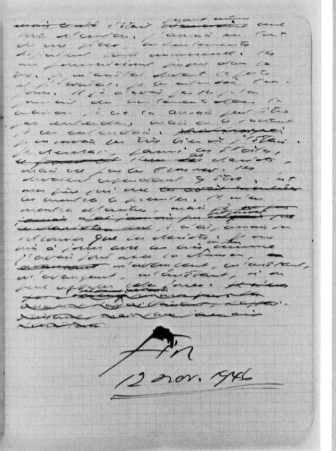

LA

"PETITE HISTOIRE"

DE L'ATTRIBUTION

DU PRIX NOBEL

A

SAMUEL BECKETT

*

PAR LE Dr. KJELL STRÖMBERG
Ancien conseiller culturel à l'Ambassade de Suède à Paris

359 364

Inscribed on the first page: "for John [Kobler] with love from Sam /
Paris Jan 1971."
The text varies from the published version.

361. *Premier Amour.* [Paris] Les Editions de Minuit (1970). 8vo, original
wrappers, uncut and unopened.

First edition. One of 106 numbered large-paper copies on *pur fil
Lafuma* of a total edition of 399.
Inscribed on the half-title: "for John [Kobler] with / love from Sam /
Paris june / 1970."

362. *First Love.* Translated from the original French by the author. London:
Calder & Boyars (1973). 8vo, original cloth, dust jacket.

First edition in English.
Inscribed on the title page: "for John & Evelyn [Kobler] / with love
from Sam / Paris oct. 1973."

363. *First Love and Other Shorts.* New York: Grove Press (1974). 8vo, original cloth, dust jacket.

This collected edition includes *First Love, From an Abandoned Work, Enough, Imagination Dead Imagine, Ping, Not I,* and *Breath.*

364. *Malone Meurt. Oh les beaux jours.* With illustrations by Avigdor Arikha and a portrait of Samuel Beckett by Michel Cauvet. [Paris] Editions Rombaldi [1971]. Small 4to, original cloth decorated with a composition in colors by Picasso.

From the *Collection des Prix Nobel de Littérature,* published with the support of the Swedish Academy and the Nobel Foundation. With a prefatory essay, "La 'Petite histoire' de l'attribution du Prix Nobel à Samuel Beckett" by Dr. Kjell Strömberg, former cultural attaché of the Swedish Embassy in Paris, and a study by John Montague, "La Vie et l'oeuvre de Samuel Beckett."

With presentation inscriptions to John and Evelyn [Kobler] from the author and the illustrator.

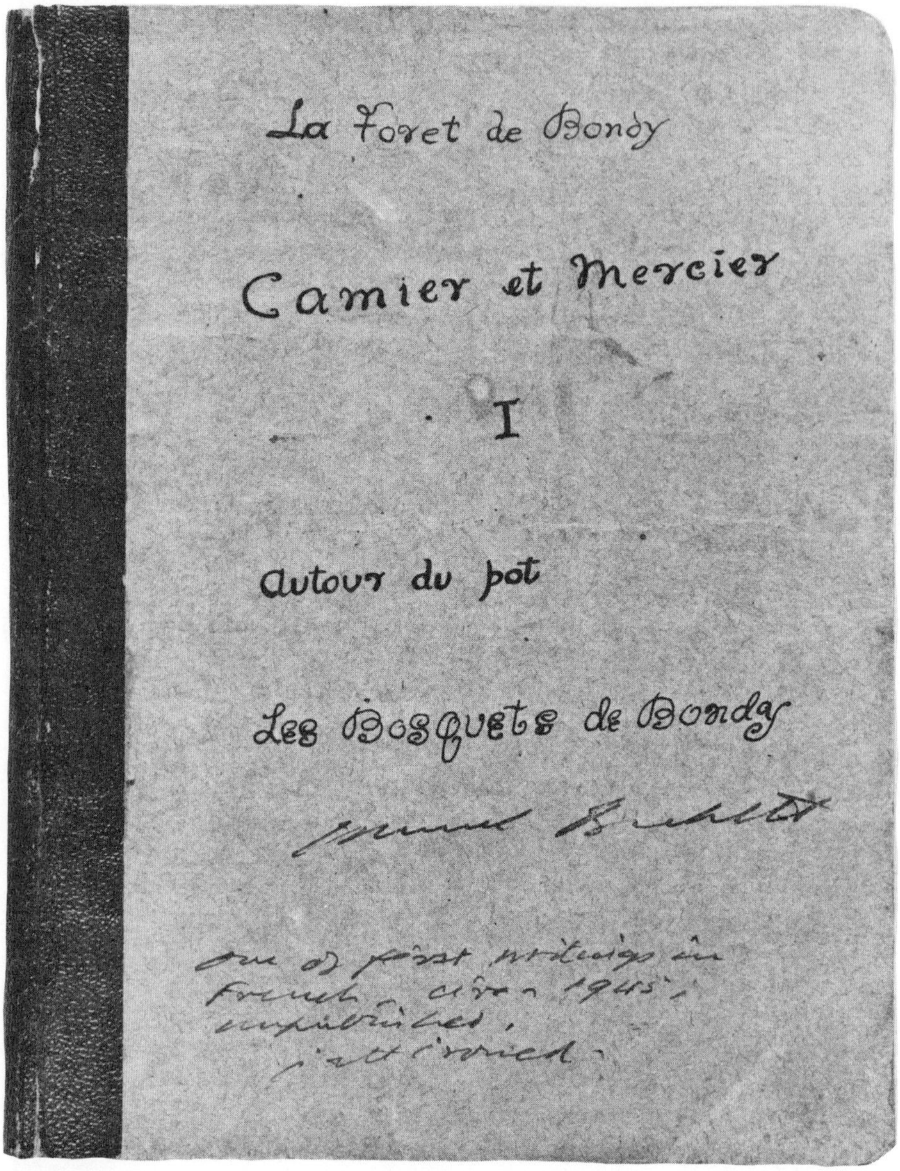

La Forêt de Bondy

Camier et Mercier

I

autour du pot

Les Bosquets de Bondy

[signature]

[handwritten note in pencil]
one of first writings in
French — circa 1945,
unpublished,
(attributed?)

365

MERCIER ET CAMIER
MERCIER AND CAMIER

Mercier et Camier, on which Beckett began work in July 1946, was his first novel written in French. Like most of Beckett's work, it is deeply autobiographical. The Paris publisher Bordas had first refusal of it under the terms of their contract for the French edition of *Murphy*, but the firm did so poorly with *Murphy* that it lost faith in Beckett's future. As late as 21 February 1959, in a letter to Reavey, Beckett was referring to *Mercier et Camier*, "a short 'novel' written before *Molloy*," as something that had been "shelved. Unpublished and unavailable." However, in 1970, after periodic prodding by Les Editions de Minuit, Beckett allowed *Mercier et Camier* to be published. In 1974, in a translation on which Beckett had worked by fits and starts over a period of three years, the novel was brought out in English by Calder & Boyars.

365. "Mercier et Camier." Autograph manuscript, signed, 1946, 329 pp. Written in blue and black inks and brown crayon in two small-4to notebooks with blue covers.

The manuscript has many revisions and there are numerous doodles and diagrams throughout. The last page of the second notebook has a draft of a letter to Simone de Beauvoir concerning Beckett's short story "Suite." (See No. 172.)

The cover of Notebook I is lettered: "La Forêt de Bondy / Camier et Mercier / I / Autour du pot / Les Bosquets de Bondy," and is signed "Samuel Beckett," with the note: "One of first writings in / French, circa 1945, / unpublished / jettisoned." The manuscript's beginning date is shown as 5 July 1946.

The cover of Notebook II is lettered: "Voyage / de / Mercier et Camier / Autour du pot / Dans / Les Bosquets de Bondy / Pairs et compagnons." The final date, at the beginning of Chapter X, is given as "Sept. 26." But the preliminary pages of the notebook containing the manuscript of Beckett's story "L'Expulsé" include the end of *Mercier et Camier*, and there the actual date of completion is given as 3 October 1946. Although Admussen states that the manuscript is "complete only through Chapter 10 (out of 12 [in the published text])," in reality it corresponds closely to the published text and is, in fact, a complete autograph version of *Mercier et Camier*.

Confusion about the manuscript's completeness arises from two sources: (1) the manuscript is continued in a third notebook—the one containing the manuscript of "L'Expulsé," which Beckett began three days after finishing *Mercier et Camier* and (2) Beckett wrote *"résumés"* of groups of chapters which are organized in a slightly different fashion in the autograph manuscript from their arrangement in the typed

Guillaume Apollinaire

Samuel Beckett

A la fin tu es las de ce monde ancien

Bergère ô tour Eiffel le troupeau des ponts bêle ce matin

Tu en as assez de vivre dans l'antiquité grecque et romaine

Ici même les automobiles ont l'air d'être anciennes
La religion seule est restée toute neuve la religion
Est restée simple comme les hangars de Port-Aviation

Seul en Europe tu n'es pas antique ô Christianisme
L'Européen le plus moderne c'est vous Pape Pie X
Et toi que les fenêtres observent la honte te retient
D'entrer dans une église et de t'y confesser ce matin
Tu lis les prospectus les catalogues les affiches qui chantent tout
    haut
Voilà la poésie ce matin et pour la prose il y a les journaux
Il y a les livraisons à 25 centimes pleines d'aventures policières
Portraits des grands hommes et mille titres divers

8

In the end you are weary of this ancient world

This morning the bridges are bleating Eiffel Tower oh herd

Weary of living in Roman antiquity and Greek

Here even the motor-cars look antique
Religion alone has stayed young religion
Has stayed simple like the hangars at Port Aviation

You alone in Europe Christianity are not ancient
The most modern European is you Pope Pius X
And you whom the windows watch shame restrains
From entering a church this morning and confessing your sins
You read the handbills the catalogues the singing posters
So much for poetry this morning and the prose is in the papers
Special editions full of crimes
Celebrities and other attractions for 25 centimes

9

370

manuscript (referred to below) and in the published book. The view becomes even cloudier as a result of Beckett's unconventional system of numbering these *résumés* as chapters. In the autograph manuscript Beckett summarizes the eight "conventional" chapters in three *résumés* (which in themselves constitute three additional chapters and bring the total chapter count to eleven). In the typed manuscript and the published version he summarizes those same eight chapters in four *résumés* (which bring the total chapter count to twelve). Contrary to Admussen's statement in his description of "L'Expulsé" (op. cit., pp. 47–48), the preliminary pages of that manuscript are not "notes pertaining to *Mercier et Camier*," but are the *résumés* for the two preceding "conventional" chapters and thus form the final chapter of both the manuscript and the book.

366. "Mercier et Camier." Photocopy of typed manuscript, 151 pp., 4to.

An autograph note on the cover in Samuel Beckett's hand reads: "Written 1947? / Never attempted English translation. / This [handwritten title page] is Judith Schmidt's hand- / writing I think. / No idea where original type- / script and ms. / Limited or normal edition / probable eventually. / Samuel Beckett / March 1969."

The "ms." referred to was then, as now, in Austin and is described under No. 365. The "limited or normal edition" was published the following year by Les Editions de Minuit (see No. 367).

367. *Mercier et Camier.* [Paris] Les Editions de Minuit (1970). 8vo, original wrappers, uncut and unopened.

First edition. One of 99 numbered large-paper copies on *pur fil Lafuma.*

Inscribed on the half-title: "for John [Kobler] with / love from Sam / Paris june 1971."

368. "Mercier and Camier." Two extracts in *Spectrum*, Vol. IV, No. 1 (Winter 1960). Goleta: University of California, Santa Barbara. 8vo, original printed wrappers.

The extracts are entitled "Madden" and "The Umbrella." Under "Contributors' Notes," the editors have written, "Our publication of two translated extracts marks the first appearance of any of [*Mercier et Camier*] in any form. Mr. Beckett is in no way responsible for the translations but has generously sanctioned their use."

Beckett's autograph signature appears at the beginning of the extracts.

369. *Mercier and Camier*. Translated from the original French by the author. London: Calder & Boyars (1974). 12mo, original boards, dust jacket. First edition in English.

370. Guillaume Apollinaire. *Zone*. With an English translation by Samuel Beckett. Dublin: The Dolmen Press and London: Calder & Boyars (1972). Small 4to, original leather-backed cloth, in publisher's slipcase.

One of 250 numbered copies signed by Samuel Beckett and specially bound.

In a letter to Jack MacGowran on 16 April 1971, Beckett wrote: "*Zone* is an old translation of a poem by Apollinaire published unsigned in *transition* in the fifties. I gave my only copy to Liam Miller for separate publication by Dolmen. I don't know when he plans to bring it out. The poem is the opening one in the collection entitled *Alcools*."

MOUTH:
(contd)

... realized ... words were coming ... words **were**
coming ... a voice she did not recognize ... at
first ... so long since it had sounded ... **then finally**
had to admit ... could be none other ... **than her**
own ... certain vowel sounds ... she had **never**
heard ... elsewhere ... so that people would stare
... the rare occasions ... once or twice a year ...
always winter some strange reason ... stare at **her**
uncomprehending ... and now this stream ...
steady stream ... she who had never ... on the
contrary ... practically speechless ... all her
days ... how she survived! ... even shopping ...
busy shopping centre ... supermart ... just handed
in the list ... with the bag ... old black shopping
bag ... then stood there waiting ... any length of
time ... middle of the throng ... motionless ...
staring into space ... mouth half open as usual ...
till it was back in her hand ... the bag back in her
hand ... then pay and go ... not as much as goodbye
... how she survived! ... 'and now this stream ...
not catching the half of it ... not the quarter ... no
idea ... what she was saying ... imagine! ... no
idea what she was saying ... till she began trying
to ... delude herself ... it was not hers at all ...
not her voice at all ... and would have no doubt ...
vital she should ... was on the point ... after long
efforts ... when suddenly she felt ... gradually she
felt ... her lips moving ... imagine! ... her lips
moving ... as of course till then she had not ...
and not alone the lips ... the cheeks ... the jaws
... the whole face ... all those - ... what? ...
the tongue? ... yes ... the tongue in the mouth
... all those contortions without which ... no speech
possible ... and yet in the ordinary way ... not
felt at all ... so intent one is ... on what one is
saying ... the whole being ... hanging on its words
... so that not only she had ... had she ... not only
had she ... to give up ... admit hers alone ... her
voice alone ... but this other awful thought ... sudden
flash ... oh long after! ... even more awful if
possible ... that feeling was coming back ... feeling
was coming back! ... starting at the top ... then
working down ... the whole machine ... but no ...
spared that ... the mouth alone ... so far ... ha!
... so far ... then thinking ... oh long after ...
sudden flash ... it can't go on ... all this ... all
that ... steady stream ... straining to hear ... make
something of it ... and her own thoughts ... make
something of them ... all - ... What? ... the buzzing?

373

154

NOT I
PAS MOI

In the work of a dramatist where the unusual is the usual, *Not I*, written in the spring of 1972, is one of the most unusual and dramatic of the Beckett canon. The light focuses on a disembodied female mouth in constant ebullition, visible at a level of about eight feet above the stage. In seventeen minutes the mouth reviews "her" three-score-and-ten, at a speed which is all but exhausting for both actress and audience. An "auditor" raises his arms from time to time "in a gesture of helpless compassion."

On Christmas Day 1972 Beckett wrote to Reavey: "Good prospects for *Not I* with Billie Whitelaw & Jocelyn Herbert's set." And on 19 January 1973: "Quite pleased with London production. B. Whitelaw marvellous in *Not I*, but [Albert] Finney quite miscast [in *Krapp's Last Tape*]. . . . Jocelyn Herbert did a great job as always."

It was more than two years before the French version—*Pas Moi*—opened. Beckett wrote Reavey on 1 September 1972, "Madeleine Renaud is to have a go at French *Not I* next March in the small theatre of the new quai d'Orsay setup." On 23 March 1975 they were "rehearsing French *Not I* with M. Renaud, with yet another *Krapp* to eke it out, opening April 8. Then farewell to theatre." And on 14 April: "*Pas Moi* off to a goodish start. Vast relief at thought of no more theatre."

371. "Not I." Photocopy of a typed manuscript corrected in Beckett's hand, 6 pp., 4to.

   This text varies substantively from both the mimeographed acting version and the proof sheets, listed below. Apparently an earlier version of the play.
   From the George Reavey Collection.

372. *Not I* and *Krapp's Last Tape*. Mimeographed acting versions. London: Royal Court Theatre [1972]. Folio, loose in sheets within red paper covers.

   The script of *Not I* does not reflect the changes made by Beckett in the Faber and Faber proof sheets, described below.

373. *Not I*. Proof sheets, signed, 1972, 9 pp., 4to.

   With a substantial number of autograph corrections, some revision, and one major deletion. An autograph note on the title page identifies the sheets as "Corrected copy for Faber / December 72." An inscription on the first page of the text reads: "for John & Evelyn [Kobler] / with love from Sam / Paris Feb. 1973."

374. *Not I*. London: Faber and Faber (1973). 12mo, original pictorial stiff wrappers.

   First edition. With one autograph deletion.
   Inscribed on the title page: "for / John and Evelyn [Kobler] / with love from Sam / Paris October 1973."
   In spite of Beckett's precise correction of the proof sheets, Faber and Faber introduced a new error, which Beckett has crossed out in ink on page 11.

   Not I. See also Nos. 363, 386, 388.

375. "Pas Moi." In *Minuit*, No. 12 (January 1975). 8vo, original pictorial wrappers.

   Pas Moi appeared in book form on 17 January.

376. *Pas Moi*. [Paris] Les Editions de Minuit (1975). 12mo, original wrappers, uncut and unopened.

   First edition of Beckett's translation of *Not I*. One of 150 numbered copies on *vélin Arches* of a total edition of 242.

377. *That Time*. Processed acting version. London: Royal Court Theatre [1975?]. Folio, loose in sheets within blue paper covers.

   "Have written a short piece (theatre): *That Time*. *Not I* family. Needs revision," Beckett wrote to George Reavey on 1 September 1974, after a long summer of writing at Ussy. As in *Not I*, where the focus is on "MOUTH . . . rest of face in shadow," here it is "Old white face" with "long flowing white hair" that dominates the stage, this time not speaking but listening to three voices from his past.

378. *That Time*. London: Faber and Faber (1976). 12mo, original wrappers, illustrated on the front cover with a photograph of Samuel Beckett by Jerry Bauer.

   First edition. The play was performed for the first time at the Royal Court Theatre in the spring of 1976 during a Samuel Beckett season celebrating the author's seventieth birthday.

379. *That Time*. In *I Can't Go On, I'll Go On*. A Selection from Samuel Beckett's Work. Edited and introduced by Richard W. Seaver. New York: Grove Press (1976). 8vo, original cloth, dust jacket. First American printing.

   That Time. See also Nos. 386, 388.

380. *Cette Fois*. Translated from the English by the author. [Paris] Les Editions de Minuit (1978). 12mo, original wrappers, uncut and un-opened. First edition in French. One of 100 numbered copies on *vélin d'Arches*.

384

Cette Fois. See also No. 413.

381. *Footfalls.* Processed acting version. London: Royal Court Theatre [1975?]. Folio, loose in sheets within black paper covers.

   Beckett wrote *Footfalls* soon after *That Time,* both of them autobiographical. *Footfalls* was written for Billie Whitelaw, who created the role in the production staged by the Royal Court Theatre in the spring of 1976 as part of their Festival celebrating Beckett's seventieth birthday.

382. *Footfalls.* London: Faber and Faber (1976). 12mo, original wrappers illustrated on the front cover with a photograph of Samuel Beckett by Jerry Bauer. First edition.

Footfalls. See also Nos. 386, 388.

383. *Pas.* [Paris] Les Editions de Minuit (1977). 12mo, original wrappers, uncut and unopened. First edition of Beckett's translation into French of *Footfalls.* One of 135 numbered copies on *vélin Arches* of a total edition of 227.

Pas. See also No. 392.

384. Samuel Beckett rehearsing *Footfalls* with Billie Whitelaw, Royal Court Theatre, London, 1976. Photograph by John Haynes.

385. "Sketch for Radio Play." In *Stereo Headphones: An Occasional Magazine of the New Poetries*, No. 7 (Spring 1976). Small 4to, original illustrated wrappers.

First appearance of this radio play, later collected as *Radio I* in *Ends and Odds*, published by Grove Press in 1976 and Faber & Faber in 1977.

The inside front cover reproduces an etching by Arikha, "Samuel Beckett Seated: 1972." The back cover has John Christie's "Molloy's Solution to the 16 [sucking] stones + Tribute Text to Samuel B. by Nicholas Zurbrugg."

386. *Ends and Odds. Eight New Dramatic Pieces.* New York: Grove Press (1976). 8vo, original cloth, dust jacket.

First collected edition.

This collection contains, as "Ends," the stage plays *Not I, That Time,* and *Footfalls,* and the television play *Ghost Trio;* as "Odds," two pieces for theatre (*Theatre I* and *Theatre II*) and two for radio (*Radio I* and *Radio II*). *Ghost Trio* is printed here for the first time in book form.

387. "Ghost Trio." In *Journal of Beckett Studies* [No. 1] (Winter 1976). 8vo, original wrappers, illustrated with a photograph by John Haynes of Samuel Beckett and Billie Whitelaw during rehearsals for the 1976 Royal Court production of *Footfalls.*

First appearance of this television play, later collected in *Ends and Odds* (Faber & Faber, 1977).

Ghost Trio was first televised on BBC 2 in the spring of 1977, as was another of Beckett's recent television plays, *. . . but the clouds. . . .* Both were directed by Donald McWhinnie; the roles in each were played by Billie Whitelaw and Ronald Pickup.

388. *Ends and Odds. Plays and Sketches.* London: Faber & Faber (1977). 12mo, original blue cloth, dust jacket illustrated with a photograph of Beckett by Jerry Bauer.

First English edition, with the same contents as the Grove Press edition except for the additional television play *. . . but the clouds . . .,* printed here for the first time.

389. "Esquisse Radiophonique." In *Minuit*, No. 5 (September 1973). Paris [Les Editions de Minuit]. 8vo, original pictorial wrappers, uncut and unopened.

One of 50 numbered copies on *vélin Arches.*

Esquisse Radiophonique was written during the last two days of November 1961 and was immediately followed by the radio play *Cascando,* to which it is related.

390. "Fragment de théâtre." In *Minuit*, No. 8 (March 1974). 8vo, original pictorial wrappers.

First appearance of this work, later collected in *Pas suivi de quatre esquisses* (1978) as *Fragment de théâtre I*.

391. "Pochade Radiophonique." In *Minuit*, No. 16 (November 1975). 8vo, original pictorial wrappers.

First appearance of this radio play, later published in *Pas suivi de quatre esquisses* (1978).

392. *Pas suivi de quatre esquisses.* [Paris] Les Editions de Minuit (1978). 12mo, original printed wrappers, uncut and unopened.

First collected edition in French. One of 86 numbered copies on *pur fil Lafuma.*

In addition to *Pas*, this collection includes four other sketches: *Fragment de théâtre I, Fragment de théâtre II, Pochade Radio-phonique (Radio II)*, and *Esquisse Radiophonique (Radio I)*.

3*/60   S W Hayter 73

397

FOIRADES
FIZZLES

The title of this group of short pieces, written originally (with one exception) in French over a period of fifteen years, is a characteristically self-deprecating gesture on Beckett's part: to wit,

    foirade: (a) squitters; (b) jitters; (c) disaster, flop

> *Harrap's New Standard French and English Dictionary* (London and Paris: Harrap, 1981)

    fizzle: 1: *archaic:* the act of breaking wind quietly
                2: hiss, sputter, fizz
                3: an abortive effort: failure, fiasco

> *Webster's Third New International Dictionary* (Springfield, Massachusetts: G. & C. Merriam, 1971)

393. "Foirade ['Il est tête nue']." In *Minuit*, No. 1 (November 1972). 8vo, original illustrated wrappers, uncut and unopened. One of 50 numbered copies on *vélin Arches*.

394. "Foirades II et III ['J'ai renoncé avant de naître' and 'Horn venait la nuit']." In *Minuit*, No. 2 (January 1973). 8vo, original illustrated wrappers, uncut and unopened. One of 50 numbered copies on *vélin Arches*.

395. "Foirades IV et V ['Vieille terre, assez menti, je l'ai vue' and 'Se voir']." In *Minuit*, No. 4 (May 1973). 8vo, original illustrated wrappers, uncut and unopened. One of 50 numbered large-paper copies on *vélin Arches*.

396. "Au loin un oiseau." Page proofs, 1973, 8 pp., small 4to.

    With autograph note and one correction by Beckett.
    Inscribed on the first page: "due soon with etchings / by Avigdor [Arikha] / for John & Evelyn [Kobler] / with love from Sam / Paris 25.8.73."

397. *Still*. With original etchings by Stanley William Hayter. [Milano] M'Arte Edizioni [1974]. Folio, loose in sheets within original green-and-white decorative wrappers, uncut. In publisher's matching slip-case.

    One of 30 numbered copies on handmade paper with two states of the etchings, one in black, the other in color. The total edition was limited to 160 copies, printed in Garamond by Stefanoni on a rag paper specially made for this edition.

Beckett's text was written for his friend Bill Hayter to illustrate and is printed here for the first time. It is accompanied by Luigi Majno's Italian translation. In addition to the bilingual typographical presentation there is a facsimile reproduction of Samuel Beckett's manuscript signed in ink by him.

Hayter's original etchings are numbered and signed in pencil by the artist and were produced in his celebrated Atelier 17, in Paris.

398. *Immobile.* Translated from the English by the author. [Paris] Les Editions de Minuit (1976). Square 12mo, original wrappers, uncut and unopened.

> One of 125 numbered copies on *vélin Arches.*
> This is Beckett's translation of *Still.*

399. *Pour finir encore.* [Paris] Les Editions de Minuit (1976). Square 12mo, original printed wrappers, uncut and unopened. First edition. One of 125 numbered copies on *vélin Arches.*

400. *Pour finir encore et autres foirades.* [Paris] Les Editions de Minuit (1976). 12mo, original printed wrappers.

> First collected edition, which includes the short prose works "Pour finir encore" ("For to end yet again"), "Immobile" ("Still"), "Il est tête nue" ("He is barehead"), "J'ai renoncé avant de naître" ("I gave up before birth"), "Horn venait la nuit" ("Horn came always"), "Vieille terre, assez menti, je l'ai vue" ("Old earth"), "Au loin un oiseau" ("Afar a Bird"), and "Se voir" ("Closed place").

401. *Foirades / Fizzles.* With original etchings by Jasper Johns. London and New York: Petersburg Press, 1976. 4to, original wrappers, uncut, in publisher's linen-bound folding case.

> The edition consists of five texts by Samuel Beckett which he wrote in French in 1972. He translated them into English in 1974 for the purposes of this edition.
>
> Jasper Johns's thirty-three original etchings were executed in 1975 and printed on the hand-press of the Atelier Crommelynck in Paris. The handmade paper from the Moulin Richard de Bas in Auvergne is watermarked with Beckett's initials and Johns's signature. The text, composed in 16-point Caslon Old Face, was hand-printed by the Paris typographers Fequet et Baudier.
>
> The interior of the book's case is lined with original lithographs in color by Jasper Johns. The edition was limited to 300 numbered copies signed by the author and the artist. The original prospectus is laid in.
>
> Beckett's first suggestion, when a collaboration with Jasper Johns was proposed to him, was that Johns do something with *Godot.* But Johns preferred to work with an unpublished text: hence *Fizzles.* Johns's etchings, based on a four-panel painting he did in 1972, called, somewhat perversely, *Untitled,* provide a very subjective counterpoint to Beckett's texts. And yet there is a kind of logic in pairing Beckett with Johns in this enterprise. In the work of each there is a constant

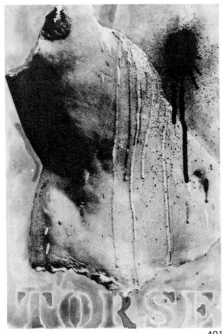

Downstream on impassive river[s s]uddenly
I felt the towline of the bo[atmen] slacken.
Redskins had taken them in a [scr]eam and stripped them and
Skewered them to the glaring [sta]kes for targets.

Then, delivered from my stra[ining] boatmen,
From the trivial racket of [trivi]al crews and from
The freights of Flemish grai[n an]d English cotton,
I made my own course down th[e pa]ssive rivers.

Blanker than the brain of a [chil]d I fled
Through winter, I scoured th[e fu]rious jolts of the tides,
In an uproar and a chaos of [Pen]insulas,
Exultant, from their moorings [in] triumph torn.

I started awake to tempestuou[s b]allowings.
Nine nights I danced like a c[ork] on the billows, I danced
On the breakers, sacrificial, [f]or ever and ever,
And the crass eye of the lant[er]ns was expunged.

More firmly bland than to chi[ld]ren apples' firm pulp,
Soaked the green water throug[b] my hull of pine,
Scattering helm and grappling [an]d washing me
Of the stains, the vomitings [an]d blue wine.

401 405

404

163

renewal of the means, a continuing inner search that brings forth an unending series of statements or images that explore but never exhaust the questions implicit in the memory or the visual stimulus to which the writer and the artist are—each in his own way—responding.

402. *For To End Yet Again and Other Fizzles.* London: John Calder (1976). 8vo, original boards, dust jacket.

First English edition, with some ambiguity in the translated title of "Se voir" ("Closed Space," "Closed place"). The same contents as *Pour finir encore et autres foirades,* in Beckett's translation, except for "Still," which he wrote originally in English.

403. *Fizzles.* New York: Grove Press (1976). 8vo, original cloth, dust jacket.

First American edition. The same text as the English edition but with the segments in a different order and titled simply "Fizzle 1" through "Fizzle 8."

404. Samuel Beckett with Jasper Johns in Paris. Photograph by Robert Doisneau.

405. *Drunken Boat.* A translation of Arthur Rimbaud's poem "Le Bateau ivre." Edited with an introduction by James Knowlson and Felix Leakey. Reading: Whiteknights Press, 1976. Folio, original cloth.

First printing of Beckett's translation. One of 100 copies in a special binding and signed by Samuel Beckett.
The book includes a facsimile of Beckett's typescript and both French and English texts. Beckett completed this translation on commission from Edward Titus in 1932, but Titus's review, *This Quarter,* suspended publication before it could be printed.

406. "Deux Poèmes." In *Minuit,* No. 33 (March 1979). 8vo, original pictorial wrappers.

First publication of these two poems, "le nain nonagénaire" and "à bout de songes un bouquin."

407. "neither." In *Journal of Beckett Studies,* No. 4 (Spring 1979). 8vo, original wrappers, illustrated with a photograph from Samuel Beckett's production of *Happy Days,* with Billie Whitelaw, at the Royal Court Theatre, 1979.

First printing, marginally mutilated by a printer's error.
Beckett wrote "neither" in September 1976 to be set to music by Morton Feldman. It was first performed at the Rome Opera in June 1977.

408. "A Piece of Monologue." In *The Kenyon Review,* Vol. I, No. 3, New Series (Summer 1979). Royal 8vo, original pictorial wrappers. First printing.

409. *Rockaby and Other Short Pieces.* New York: Grove Press (1981). 8vo, original cloth, dust jacket.

First edition, containing *Rockaby, Ohio Impromptu, All Strange Away,* and *A Piece of Monologue.*

A Piece of Monologue was written for David Warrilow (of the Mabou Mines Company) and was first performed, by him, in New York in 1979. *Rockaby* was written for a seminar in Buffalo in 1981 and was played by Billie Whitelaw and directed by Alan Schneider. *Ohio Impromptu,* written for a seminar at Ohio State University in 1981, was played by David Warrilow and Rand Mitchell and directed by Alan Schneider. The text *All Strange Away* was first published in 1976 by Gotham Book Mart (see No. 320).

410. *Three Occasional Pieces.* [London] Faber and Faber (1982). 12mo, original wrappers, front cover illustrated with a photograph of Beckett by Christina Burton.

First English edition, having the same contents as *Rockaby and Other Short Pieces,* except for *All Strange Away.*

411. "Solo (Piece of Monologue)." Typed manuscript signed, 4 pp., folio.

With substantial revision, mostly in the form of deletions and some additions, in red and black inks and in pencil. Contains a number of variants from the published version and appears to be a later type-script, but not the final one.

This typescript is particularly interesting in that it reveals Beckett's method of "translating" *A Piece of Monologue* into French. He begins with a literal rendering of the text from English into French, with as many as three alternative choices of phrasing, varying in length from one word to an entire sentence, within parentheses and underlined sometimes in red ink, sometimes in black. He then eliminates the rejected alternatives and further reduces the text, through deletion, so that rather than being a strict translation, *Solo* becomes an adaptation of the original work.

411a. *Solo suivi de Catastrophe.* [Paris] Les Editions de Minuit (1982). 12mo, original wrappers, uncut and unopened.

First edition. One of 99 numbered copies on *vélin d'Arches.*
Solo is Beckett's adaptation into French of *A Piece of Monologue.* *Catastrophe,* written in French, is dedicated to Vaclav Havel, the Czechoslovak playwright who had been imprisoned for his activity in behalf of the human-rights section of the 1975 Helsinki Agreement.

412. *Berceuse suivi de Impromptu d'Ohio.* Translated from the original English by the author. [Paris] Les Editions de Minuit (1982). 12mo, original printed wrappers, uncut and unopened. First edition in French of Samuel Beckett's translations of *Rockaby* and *Ohio Impromptu.* One of 99 numbered large-paper copies.

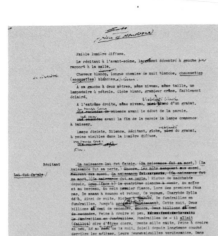

411 414

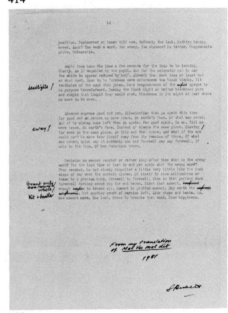

420

413. *Catastrophe et autres dramaticules.* [Paris] Les Editions de Minuit (1982). 12mo, original printed wrappers, uncut and unopened. First collected edition, including *Cette Fois, Solo, Berceuse,* and *Impromptu d'Ohio.* One of 100 numbred copies on *vélin supérieur.*

414. ["Company"]. Typed manuscript (incomplete), 1979, 2 pp., 4to.

   With extensive autograph revisions, deletions, and additions in red and black inks, giving evidence of Beckett's having returned to the text on a number of different occasions. An inscription, in his hand, at the bottom of the second page reads: "End of first typescript of *Company* / (provisional title). / Paris 27.7.79."
   This two-page typescript, the last pages of the first typed draft of *Company,* corresponds to the last six pages of the English edition. The typescript varies substantially from the published text. Beckett has deleted the closing lines and replaced them with a passage that comes nearer to the finished version.

415. "Heard in the Dark 2." In *Journal of Beckett Studies,* No. 5 (Autumn 1979). 8vo, original illustrated wrappers. The photograph on the cover is of the 1978 German production of *Come and Go* at the Schiller-Theater.

   Prepublication extract from *Company,* with variants.
   In this extract, as in so many of Beckett's works, mathematical calculations function in a variety of ways. They lend precision and often add a touch of dry humor to a text. They become a means of passing time. Or, as the protagonist in this passage from "Heard in the Dark 2" states: "Simple sums you find a help in times of trouble. A haven. . . . Even still in the timeless dark you find figures a comfort."

416. *Company.* London: John Calder (1980). 12mo, original black cloth, dust jacket. First English edition.

417. *Company.* New York: Grove Press (1980). 8vo, original cloth-backed boards, dust jacket. First American edition.

418. *Compagnie.* [Paris] Les Editions de Minuit [1980]. Square 12mo, original printed wrappers, uncut and unopened. First edition of the author's French translation of *Company.* One of 106 numbered copies on *Alfamousse.*

419. *Mal vu mal dit.* [Paris] Les Editions de Minuit [1981]. Square 12mo, original printed wrappers, uncut and unopened. First edition. One of 114 numbered copies on *Alfamousse.*

420. ["Ill Seen Ill Said"]. Typed manuscript (incomplete), signed, 1981, 5 pp., folio.

   With autograph revisions throughout, in black inks.
   This typescript includes paragraphs 22–26, 31–33, and 47–61 (the

final fifth of the book) and shows many variants from the published text.

An inscription on the last page reads: "From my translation / of *Mal vu mal dit* / 1981 / S. Beckett."

421. "Ill Seen Ill Said." In *The New Yorker* (October 5, 1981). 4to, original illustrated wrappers.

First appearance of *Mal vu mal dit* in English. Translated from the French by the author.

422. *Ill Seen Ill Said.* Translated from French by the author. New York: Grove Press (1981). 8vo, original wrappers. First edition.

423. *Ill Seen Ill Said.* Northridge: Lord John Press, 1982. Square 12mo, calf-backed marbled boards, gilt fillets. One of 299 numbered copies, signed by the author. Designed and printed in two colors in Bembo type on mouldmade Bugrabutten. Binding by Bela Blau.

424. *Ill Seen Ill Said.* Translated from French by the author. London: John Calder (1982). 8vo, original cloth-backed boards, dust jacket. First English edition.

425. "Un Soir." In *Minuit*, No. 37 (January 1980). 8vo, original pictorial wrappers.

First printing of a short prose work which may have been an early draft leading toward *Mal vu mal dit*. Although "Un Soir" stands independently and is more explicit, it contains numerous elements of *Mal vu mal dit* (published in 1981)—e.g., an old woman dressed in black, a figure lying on the ground, the whiteness of hair and skin, flowers, the pasture, lambs, the time of day (evening), the tomb—and seems to be related to the longer piece in much the way *All Strange Away* is to *Imagination Dead Imagine* and *Le Dépeupleur* to *Bing*.

426. "One Evening." In *Journal of Beckett Studies*, No. 6 (Autumn 1980). 8vo, original illustrated wrappers. The cover photograph, by Anneliese Heuer, is of the 1978 German production of *That Time*, performed at the Schiller-Theater. First printing of "Un Soir" in its English translation.

427. *Worstward Ho.* London: John Calder (1983). Small 8vo, original green cloth, dust jacket.

First edition.
A highly condensed short prose text, in the tradition of *All Strange Away, Imagination Dead Imagine*, and *Ill Seen Ill Said*.

428. *Worstward Ho.* New York: Grove Press (1983). 8vo, original cloth-backed boards, dust jacket with an illustration by Alberto Giacometti. First American edition.

429. *Quoi Où.* [Paris] Les Editions de Minuit (1983). 8vo, original printed wrappers, uncut and unopened. First edition. One of 99 numbered copies on *vélin d'Arches.*

430. *Disjecta. Miscellaneous Writings and a Dramatic Fragment.* Edited with a foreword by Ruby Cohn. London: John Calder (1983). 12mo, original boards, dust jacket.

First collected edition. The "dramatic fragment" of the subtitle is a finished portion of "Human Wishes," an otherwise uncompleted four-act "fantasy" Beckett worked at in 1937 based on the relationship between Dr. Johnson and Mrs. Thrale.

With a presentation inscription on the title page and corrections in Beckett's hand on the final page of text.

431. "Ceiling." Autograph manuscript, signed, 1981, 8 pp., loose sheets removed from a spiral-bound notebook, 8vo.

Six consecutive versions of a short, unpublished prose piece written for the painter Avigdor Arikha and concerned with the nature of perception. Heavily revised and having numerous deletions, these drafts explore states of consciousness from the point of view of one who finds in an expanse of white a stimulus for introspection as he emerges from the "dim consciousness" of sleep to awareness.

On page 7, Beckett has written "Courmayeur / 10.7.81" and then drawn a line to separate from the earlier versions (some of them not yet fully developed) a new draft of the complete text, which begins below the line. On page 8 he indicates the date of completion for this last text as "Paris / 26.7.81." In a different shade of black ink he has written on the final page, "Samuel Beckett / July 81 unpublished." A description of the various draft versions of "Ceiling" follows:

(a) Incomplete text, untitled, written in black ink. The title, "Ceiling," has been added in the upper left corner, apparently at a later date, with a different pen. This first draft has numerous deletions and some additions. There are interesting lines in this version which are reminiscent of the opening paragraph of *Molloy* and which Beckett eliminates in the third draft: "Two pages they said. No more. After the last page two pages. Two more. No more." Within this draft Beckett has written two sets of instructions: "(Finish with '2 pages. No more.')," which he follows for one draft only, and "Insert *on* or equivalent," which he incorporates in all the subsequent drafts. This first autograph version differs considerably from the final one, particularly in its direct focus on the writing as well as on emerging consciousness:

Here so far four [pages]. ~~One~~ the coming to. ~~Two~~ the consciousness thereof. ~~Three~~ the eyes. ~~Four~~ the white.
One the coming to. Assured of no answer ~~the questions~~
hideous
~~arise. To where. From~~ and so without their ~~gruesome~~ marks the questions arise. To ~~wherever~~ where. From where. To himself.

The entire draft has been crossed out.

(b) Incomplete draft, a modified and expanded version of the preceding one, containing the basic ideas of the "finished" work. With many revisions and deletions. One long addition becomes, with further revision and expansion, the third paragraph of Typescript I (see No. 432). Here Beckett eliminates the passage quoted under (a). He retains in revised form, at the end, the lines "Two pages more. No more. After the last page two more. No more."
All parts of the draft have been crossed out.

(c) Incomplete draft, a variant of the previous one. With a few insertions, deletions, and revisions, and one long addition. Here Beckett experiments with the format of the piece, regrouping sentences into smaller paragraphs and periodically inserting—in accordance with his instructions to himself in the first autograph draft—the word "on." Although "Ceiling" here approaches its final version in both content and form, it still varies considerably from the completed work.
All parts of this draft have been crossed out.

(d) Incomplete draft, showing evidence of further experimentation with format. (Beckett has compressed the material in the previous draft into one paragraph.) With several deletions and additions. This version gives evidence, as well, of a title prior to "Ceiling"—"On coming to"—which has been deleted.
The draft has been crossed out.

(e) The last draft written at Courmayeur and complete as far as the work's overall content is concerned. It does contain material, however, which Beckett deletes in the sixth and final version. This fifth version is the most heavily worked-over of the drafts done at Courmayeur.
Appearing in this fifth autograph version, but not in the sixth and final one, nor in the subsequent typescripts, is the line "A patch of ceiling"—significant in that it is the only passage in which a direct link exists between the text and the title, thus reinforcing Beckett's emphasis on awakening and consciousness ("Dimly conscious with eyes closed of having come partly to") and the sight one first encounters upon awakening—the ceiling.
All parts of the draft have been crossed out except for the beginning portion of the third paragraph.

(f) Complete text, final autograph draft of "Ceiling," written in Paris. With deletions, additions, and word counts in the margin. In this version there is a switch from the past tense to the present, which lends immediacy to the text.

432. "Ceiling." Three typed manuscripts, 3 pp., folio.

Three typescript versions of "Ceiling," numbered 1, 2, and 3 by Beckett in the upper right-hand corner. The first typescript, which is untitled, has a number of revisions, mostly deletions, but some additions, and is a modified version of the last autograph draft of

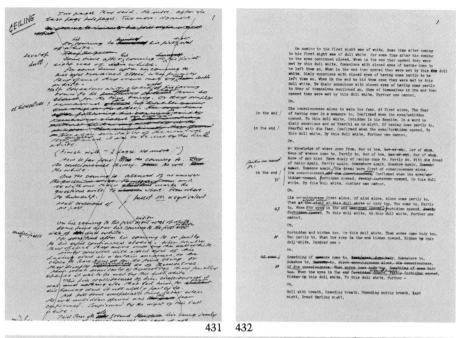

431 432

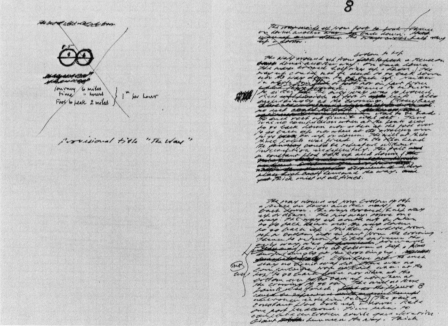

433

"Ceiling" completed at Courmayeur (see No. 431). There are word counts in the left-hand margin.

The second typescript, which is titled, corresponds (except for a few changes) to the final corrected autograph version, which was written in Paris. It has several revisions in Beckett's hand and represents a more advanced, and condensed, stage of composition.

The third typescript, also titled, reflects the changes Beckett made in the second typescript and has one new revision.

433. "The Way" ["provisional title"]. Autograph manuscript, 1981, 7 pp., removed from a spiral-bound notebook, 8vo.

Seven consecutive versions of a short piece—unpublished—describing the nature of a journey whose route circumscribes the figure 8. Beckett has written on page 1, with a pen different from the one used in the manuscript's composition: "Provisional title, 'The Way.'" The first page has, also, a diagram (and accompanying calculations) relating to the journey when its path traces the contours of a figure 8 lying on its side. Beckett has indicated that the manuscript versions which correspond to the diagram appear on page 5 (i.e., 7—the last page of the autograph manuscript).

The first four drafts, which Beckett has dated "Ussy 14.5.81," describe "the way" as it "[winds] up from foot to peak" (or "from bottom to top") and crosses midway without retracing its path, thus forming the figure 8 in its normal position. The text of the last three drafts, dated by Beckett "Ussy may 1981," differs from that of the first four, and describes the journey when its route traces an 8 lying on its side—"forth and back across a barren same winding way." The fact that Beckett begins two of the last three drafts with "or" raises the question of whether he may be considering an alternative text. A description of each of the versions follows:

(a) Complete draft, titled or subtitled "8," but with the figure apparently added later, in a different ink. With one false start and extensive revisions, additions, and deletions. The text varies markedly from the final typescript version but contains the essential ideas of the work.

The entire draft has been crossed out.

(b) Complete draft of "8," but untitled, with a number of additions and deletions. As in the preceding draft, most of the work's ideas are present, but in rough form.

The draft has been crossed out.

(c) Complete draft, untitled, with extensive revisions, deletions, and additions. The text varies substantially from both the final autograph version and the third and final typed one.

The entire draft has been crossed out.

(d) Complete draft of "8," now so titled. In the earlier, untitled drafts, Beckett seemed to be making, within the text itself, an explicit correlation between the journey he describes and the figure 8. In this version, he deletes those references, uses the figure 8 as a title, and lets the reader discover the relationship for himself. This autograph version has only two deletions and one revision and is the draft on which the first typescript is based.

(e) Incomplete draft, untitled, of the "alternative" text—"∞"—with one deletion and one revision. This is essentially a jotting down, in several lines, of the work's central idea, quickly abandoned for fuller development in the next draft. The diagram on page 1, referred to earlier, relates to this text and the two that follow. The correlation between the figure 8 lying on its side and the mathematical sign for infinity is one that Beckett introduces explicitly in the early drafts ("From figure of 8 unbroken infinitely. A legend.") and implicitly in the later ones.

(f) Complete draft of "∞," so titled, with frequent deletions and a few additions. Varies somewhat from the final autograph version.
This draft, as well as the previous fragment, has been crossed out.

(g) Complete draft of "∞," with deletions, additions, and revisions. The margin contains a reference to "Gideon," not incorporated into the text. Except for a few variants, this is the draft which appears in the third typescript.

8

The way wound up from foot to top and thence on down another way. On back down. The ways crossed midway more and less. A little more and less than midway up and down. The ways were one-way. No retracing the way up back down nor back up the way down. Neither in whole from top or foot nor in part from on the way. The one way back was on and on was always back. Freedom once at foot and top to pause or not. Before on back up and down. Briefly once at the extremes the will set free. Gait down as up same plod always. A foot a second or mile and hour and more. So from foot and top to crossways could the seconds have been numbered then height known and depth. Could but those seconds have been numbered. Thorns hemmed the way. The ways. Same mist always. Same half-light. As were the earth at rest. Loose sand underfoot. So no sign of remains no sign that none before. No one ever before so –

∞

Forth and back across a barren same winding one-way way. Low in the west or east the sun standstill. As if the earth at rest. Long shadows before and after. Same pace and countless time. Same ignorance of how far. Same leisure once at either end to pause or not. At either groundless end. Before back forth or back. Through emptiness the beaten ways as fixed as if enclosed. Were the eye to look unending void. In unending ending or beginning light. Bedrock underfoot. So no sign of remains a sign that none before. No one ever before so –

434

173

434. "The Way" ["provisional title"]. Three typed manuscripts, 3 pp. (third typescript, carbon copy), folio.

Three successive typescripts of "The Way," ["provisional title"]. The first typescript is a modified form of the fourth autograph version of "8," described above, with a substantial number of revisions in red and black inks.

The second typescript, also of the "8" section, incorporates the changes made in Typescript I and has two additional corrections and one organizational change, in black ink.

The third typescript contains both "8" and "∞," suggesting that the two pieces, rather than being "alternative" texts, are, in fact, companion pieces which describe a single journey from two perspectives: two views that finally converge on a single conclusion, stated identically in the closing sentence of each piece ("No one ever before so—").

In Typescript III, the "8" passage does not reflect the organizational change (and repeats one of the typographical errors) made in Typescript II. The "∞" segment of Typescript III is, indeed, derived from the final autograph version of that segment but shows evidence of an intermediate revision between the final manuscript version and the typescript. The fact that Typescript III alone is a carbon copy and without markings would suggest the presence, elsewhere, of the ribbon copy of Typescript III with, very likely, additional revisions by the author.

In this piece, as in "Ceiling," one comes to appreciate, through successive rereadings, the matchless precision of Beckett's method of composition. He is one of the most skilled practitioners of the craft who ever wrote. His wholly original style, unerringly true, is of the kind that "can come forth by nothing but by prayer and fasting." Which, freely translated, means by rewriting. There have been other great writers—Proust, Céline, for example—who were obsessive rewriters. But Beckett, a greater craftsman than either, goes a step beyond. His work, as these and other of his manuscripts show, is fired and purified like molten gold in the crucible. It is not surprising that all of his writing shows a precision, a concentration, and, in the broadest sense of the word, a purity which set him apart from his peers.

And here, in one short piece—"The Way"—is the distillation of all the journeys made by all of Beckett's eternal wanderers.

INDEX

175

AFTERWORD

An enterprise of this scope is nearly always the product of the combined efforts of many. It would be difficult to single out everyone who has contributed to the catalogue and the exhibition, but special recognition should be given to Decherd Turner for his unfailing support and wise counsel from the beginning; to Ellen Dunlap for vigorous logistical help at the start; to John Kirkpatrick for his shrewd winnowing of a mass of ancillary documents; to James Stroud and his colleagues of the Conservation Department for careful readying of the materials in the exhibition; to Eric Beggs for his painstaking approach to the demands of the photography; to Mary Beth Bigger and Bob Bassett for easing our way into the age of electronics; to David Price for his sure sense of design and his abundant patience; to Sally Leach for her imaginative handling of ever so many complex problems; to Linda Eichhorn for unremitting dedication to all aspects of the catalogue's preparation and for her close reading of Samuel Beckett's manuscripts—a considerable achievement, blended of persistence and percipience, which has helped to remove a number of hand-me-down misconceptions. And finally, to Samuel Beckett, whose confidence, accessibility, and quiet encouragement have done much to make an otherwise exacting job a very enjoyable one throughout.

C. L.

This volume has been printed on Warren Old Style.
The type is Trump.
Design by DAVID PRICE.